Illinois

Illinois by Road

Celebrate the States

Illinois

Marlene Targ Brill

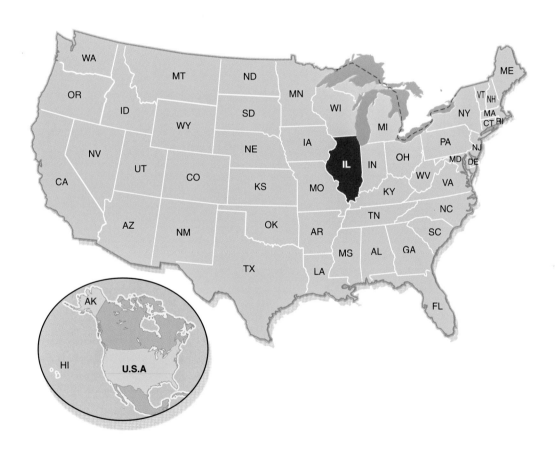

Marshall Cavendish
Benchmark
New York

Marshall Cavendish Benchmark
99 White Plains Road
Tarrytown, New York 10591-9001
www.marshallcavendish.us

All Internet sites were correct and accurate when sent to press.

Library of Congress Cataloging-in-Publication Data
Brill, Marlene Targ.
Illinois / Marlene Targ Brill.
p. cm. — (Celebrate the states) —2nd ed.
Summary: Discusses the geographic features, history, government, people,
and attractions of the state known as the Land of Lincoln.
Includes bibliographical references and index.
ISBN 0–7614–1735–4
1. Illinois—Juvenile literature. [1. Illinois.] I. Title. II. Series.
F541.3.B74 2004
977.3—dc22
2003014925

Series redesign by Adam Mietlowski

Photo research by Candlepants Incorporated
Cover photo: Susan Day/Daybreak Imagery
The photographs in this book are used by permission and through the courtesy of: *Daybreak Imagery:* Susan Day, 8, 13; Richard Day, 10, 15, 94,111, 115, 118 (both). *Animals Animals/Earth Scenes:* Lynn Stone, 14; John Lemker, 18. *Odyssey Photos, Chicago:* Kevin Mooney, 16, 63, 68, 125, back cover; Robert Frerck, 106. *The Image Works:* Frozen Images, 20; Journal-Courier, 22, 52, 92; David Frazier, 25; Journal-Courier/Steve Warmowski, 32, 65, 76, 84, 123; Zbigniew Bzdak, 59; Tannen Maury, 61, 99. *Peabody Museum, Harvard University:* (photo #T2377) 27. *Smithsonian American Museum, Washington, D.C./Art Resource, NY.* 29. *Abraham Lincoln Presidential Library/Illinois State Historical Library:* 31, 33, 36, 37, 47, 58. *Corbis:* Bettmann, 34, 41, 45, 126, 127, 131; Corbis, 39; Chuck Savage, 66; Brooks Kraft, 73; Reuters, 74, 130; Ralf Finn-Hestoft, 104; Richard Cummins, 110; Richard A. Cooke, 112. Stephane Cardinale/ People Avenue, 132. *SuperStock:* Richard Cummins, 48. *Index Stock Imagery:* Mark Segal, 50; Terri Froelich, 109. *Getty Images:* Don Smetzer, 55; Vito Palmisano, 78; Jonathon Kirn, 80; Digital Vision, 86; Andy Sacks, 89; Mark Joseph, 91; Peter Pearson, 101. *Envision:* Peter Johansky, 85.

Printed in China
3 5 6 4 2

Contents

Illinois Is . . .

Illinois is unique landscapes . . .

"I loved the prairie, the trees, flowers, and sky were thrilling by contrast."
—architect Frank Lloyd Wright

. . . and inventive people.

"Eli Sullivan called his company the Bridge Company because no one wanted to fund the new idea of a Ferris wheel."
—Becky Todd, Eli Bridge Company

"We felt very strongly that wherever people are, art and culture should be."
—Mexican Fine Arts Center Museum founder Helen Valdez

The land bore riches . . .

"On the very day of [a settler's] arrival, he could put his plow into the ground."
—explorer Father Jacques Marquette

. . . and became the nation's heartland.

"There is a power in this nation greater than either the North or the South. . . . That power is the country known as the Valley of the Mississippi, . . . the heart and soul of the nation and continent."
—U.S. senator Stephen Douglas

Some people have looked out only for themselves.

"Politicians are . . . at least one long step removed from honest men."
—state legislator Abraham Lincoln

"Everybody's out for the buck." —author Nelson Algren

Many more battled great odds to improve life in their state . . .

"American slavery and American liberty cannot co-exist on the same soil."
—Illinois College professor Truman Post

"Pray for the dead and fight like hell for the living."
—nineteenth-century champion of working people, Mary "Mother" Jones

. . . and take pride in coming from Illinois.

"People, always the people, stubborn, bitter, beautiful in their towns
and tattered farms. This is folk America, the region from which our
democratic customs, industries, and arts continuously emerge."
—historian Baker Brownell

"I hate when people say el-an-oy or illi-noise."
—children's author Charlotte Herman

*Illinois is one of our nation's best-kept secrets. Few people, even those
born in Illinois, realize how many treasures are hidden here—from
forested cliffs and mighty rivers to sleepy mining towns and lively cities.
Illinoisans work hard to build and strengthen the state they love. This
is their story. This is the story of the place they call home: Illinois.*

Chapter One

Crossroads of America

About two million years ago, more than twenty powerful glaciers crept across the land we now call Illinois. As they inched along, they sliced off hilltops and filled in steep valleys. They carved out the broad, flat land that would become the future state.

Over time, the climate grew warmer. As the earth thawed and dried, layers of crushed rock and clay that were left from the glaciers blended with plant and animal remains. The mixture turned into a mineral-rich topsoil. For centuries, settlers would come to live off this fertile land.

FLATLANDS, FORESTS, AND CANYONS

Illinois is one of twelve states making up the nation's Midwest region. Indiana lies to the east, with Iowa to the west and Wisconsin to the north. The state's southwestern neighbor is Missouri, while Kentucky borders to the southeast. Tall and thin, Illinois stretches from the country's southern region to the heart of the North. This accounts for the state's range of climate and plant and animal life.

Cypresses are evergreens that sprout thousands of needles. They thrive in the warmer climate of southern Illinois.

The Illinois prairie is dotted with a variety of flowering plants with names—such as blazing stars and rattlesnake master—as colorful as their blooms.

Much of Illinois is flatter than any of the other prairie states. It was the first prairie region reached by European explorers, who were struck by its unusual beauty. French explorer Father Jacques Marquette wrote in the late 1600s: "We have seen nothing like this river [Illinois] that we enter, as regards its fertility of soil, its prairies and woods."

At the time, grasslands covered more than half the territory. The greatest stretches of prairie spread over the state's central and northern regions. Their colorful grasses reached a variety of heights. Meadows of short yellow blades hid foxes and squirrels, while gophers and badgers lived in secret underground dens. In other parts of the prairie, wild orchids could be found tucked between the Indian yellow and the big bluestem grasses that grew to 6 feet tall by summer. The grasses helped to feed large numbers of bison, elk, and wolves, as well as white-tailed deer, the state animal.

"There are prairies three, six, ten or twenty leagues in length, and three in width surrounded by forests of the same extent; beyond these the prairies begin again," wrote Louis Jolliet, who led Marquette's expedition.

Before the arrival of settlers, trees shaded about 40 percent of Illinois. Scattered forests clustered into thick groves that divided the mostly tall, wet grasslands into smaller patches of prairie. That is why many Illinois communities have the word *grove* in their name. Long Grove and River Grove are just two examples.

Over time, settlers turned these rich prairies into farmland. Illinois poet Vachel Lindsay describes the loss of these vast stretches of land:

The tossing, blooming, perfumed grass
Is swept away by wheat,
Wheels and wheels and wheels spin by
In the spring that still is sweet.
But the flower-fed buffaloes of the spring
Left us long ago.

Although much of the original prairie has been lost since early farming days, pieces of it are now being preserved, restored, and rebuilt around the state. Some are small patches of prairie grasses and flowers found in parks and along railroad tracks and highways, while others include hundreds of acres. At 2,537 acres, Goose Lake Prairie near Morris is the state's largest natural grassland.

State leaders encourage Illinoisans to protect and honor their prairie heritage. In 1989 a contest for the finest prairie plant was held in fifty schools and colleges around Illinois. More than four thousand students chose the big bluestem as the official state prairie grass. The big bluestem grows from April through August. Its flowering stalks can reach 8 feet high, while its roots can burrow between 8 and 10 feet into the ground.

These deep roots allow the grass to thrive during times of drought. The bluestem's great height and ability to survive gave rise to the nickname "prince of the prairie."

But Illinois is more than just miles of waving grasslands. In the north-western part of the state, flatland turns into rolling hills separated by shallow valleys. White birches and mossy wetlands shelter ducks, geese, and bald eagles, our national bird. The highest point in Illinois, the 1,235-foot Charles Mound near Galena, is also found there.

Southern Illinois brings more surprises. Drivers heading south on Interstate 57 find that the flatland ends. "The endless fields of corn and soybeans almost put me to sleep," said Richard Benjamin. "It's great to find rolling hills and then trees. When we left the highway we even discovered groves of fruit trees covering the hills."

Farther south, jagged rocks jut from the earth. The rugged sandstone cliffs of the Shawnee Hills form breathtaking canyons. This mountainous region, which extends from Missouri's Ozark Mountains, is called the Illinois Ozarks. The mountains stretch 70 miles from east to west across the southern portion of the state. They include the state's greatest and most varied amount of natural resources.

The view from the 300-million-year-old rocks takes in sweeping dense forests. The surrounding Shawnee National Forest covers 268,400 acres of southern Illinois. Tupelo and cypress trees line the swamps below, where beavers, muskrats, and otters live.

The earliest pioneers in the Illinois Ozarks discovered natural salt and coal deposits beneath the earth's surface. Once miners sapped these minerals, they moved farther north. Other settlers cut timber and grew cotton. By the mid-1900s, the federal and state governments realized they had to act fast to preserve the region's rugged beauty. So they developed parks, lakes, wildlife refuges, and scenic overlooks. Now the region attracts people who love to camp, bird-watch, and fish.

Lush forests and unusual rock formations make the Garden of the Gods in the Shawnee National Forest one of the state's most scenic spots.

In 1818 nearly one-fourth of Illinois was covered with wetland. Farming and mining claimed much of this land. Today, only 2.6 percent of the state is made up of swamps and bottomland forests. More than one hundred kinds of plants and animals make their home there, including the endangered prairie chicken.

Before the mid-1800s, southeastern Chicago boasted the largest wetland in the Great Lakes region. The Calumet Region, as it was called, featured open marshland and a prime location along Lake Michigan. The area seemed ideal for Chicago's ever-expanding industry. By the mid-1900s, it was dotted with steel mills and factories. All of this development quickly became a problem, though. Many companies dumped their waste products into the wetlands, even after national laws prohibited the practice. The result was polluted wetland soil and groundwater that threatened human health and the environment for miles around. In the 1990s, city, state, and federal governments banded together to remove pollution from several sites. But the Calumet Region was so polluted by then, the cleanup proved difficult.

Kids do their part to reduce pollution and to restore natural areas. In 2002 the Illinois Environmental Protection Agency (EPA) presented its Illinois Green Youth awards to nine student groups and to one individual, Sarah Gillespie of Newton. She received the award for her successful wetland project. She built two wetlands behind her house in the hope that a variety of plants and animals will make the area their home.

These young Illinoisans help put a brighter face on their state by aiding the cleanup effort along the shore of a pond.

MYSTERIOUS CAVES

Monroe County in southern Illinois has more than one hundred caves. They are carved out of the limestone that is found underground. As water seeps into the ground, it picks up chemicals from the soil and turns acidic, like vinegar. The acid then eats into the limestone, causing it to crack. Over the years, these cracks widen to form large holes and eventually caves.

Hidden inside the caves are many unusual animals. Bats, salamanders, fish, and spiders all live in the darkness. Birds and mammals stay near the mouths of the caves. Some larger caves, such as Cave-in-Rock along the Ohio River, were once used as hideouts by pirates.

Illinois is a great place for people who like to fish. This father and son test their luck on a lake in the Crab Orchard National Wildlife Refuge.

TAMING THE WATERS

The greatest gift left by the glaciers are the state's clear, fresh bodies of water. Illinois's network of waterways has helped turn the state into one of the nation's transportation hubs. Long before settlers arrived, the Hopewell and Iliniwek traveled these waterways to trade with other native peoples. The first European pioneers cleared trees, planted grains, and mined along the Mississippi and Kaskaskia rivers. Today cities and factories depend on the state's lakes, rivers, and streams for drinking water, recreation, and shipping. "Our lakes are among our most prized natural resources," said Renee Cipriano, director of the Illinois EPA.

The Mississippi, the country's longest river, creates a natural border running the length of western Illinois. The Ohio River runs down the state's southeastern side. Both rivers come together at the state's southern tip in Cairo, an area often called Little Egypt.

Legend says the towns of Cairo and Thebes were named after the great cities of the ancient Egyptian empire. To some, the region suggested the country where the Nile River, like the Mississippi and Ohio rivers, enriched the soil along its banks. To further support the comparison, northern Illinois counties often had little rain during parts of the early 1800s, and wheat fields dried up. But in southern counties, rain fell and crops were plentiful. Author Baker Brownell wrote, "From the north came people seeking corn and wheat as to Egypt of old."

Lakes are another feature of the Illinois landscape. Lake Michigan connects northeastern Illinois with the other Great Lakes, which in turn are linked to the St. Lawrence River and the Atlantic Ocean. When settlers arrived, the lake's natural shoreline offered no harbors. So they created the large harbors at Chicago and Waukegan that remain today.

The Illinois River runs across the state to the northeast. One branch originally began about 3 miles short of the Chicago River, which flowed into Lake Michigan. Native Americans carried canoes overland between the two waterways. In 1848 Illinoisans completed a canal joining branches of the two water routes, and a swampy fur-trading settlement named Chicago exploded into a major trading center. Chicago became the nation's only inland city to link a lake, river, and ocean.

Before 1887 the Chicago River, full of waste from outhouses and industry, flowed into the lake. Hundreds of Chicagoans died of diseases after drinking this filthy river water, which had entered the lake. So engineers decided to change the direction of the river's flow. They dug the south branch deeper, which caused the water to change its course and flow west and south away from Lake Michigan. From then on, the Chicago River was called the "river that flows backward."

Illinois has another 282,000 acres of ponds and lakes as well as 430 rivers. They offer endless fun for anyone who likes to canoe, camp, and fish. The waterways teem with crappie, walleye, and perch. Bald cypress and sycamore trees line their banks.

The largest group of lakes is in Chain O'Lakes State Park, northwest of Chicago. Carlyle Lake in southern Illinois is the state's largest human-made waterway. It covers 26,000 acres and includes 83 miles of shoreline.

Perhaps the state's strangest waterway is Rend Lake. Its Y shape was created by damming the Big Muddy and Casey Fork rivers. The lake is along the Mississippi Flyway, the migration route for thousands of Canada geese and ducks. Bald eagles live here year-round.

Illinoisans value their waterways, which are often hard to protect. One threat has arrived in the form of zebra mussels, which originally came from the Caspian Sea, found between Europe and Asia. These 1- to 2-inch, stripe-shelled creatures attach to almost any hard surface, including boats.

Zebra mussels attach to boats and are then brought to new habitats. Some Illinois waterways have been invaded by these shelled creatures.

They multiply so fast that they can quickly take over freshwater habitats, filling 1 square yard with as many as 60,000 mussels and clogging water pipes and areas where fish spawn. Another problem is the large amounts of plankton, tiny plants and animals found in the water. Zebra mussels eat the plankton and convert them into waste products. A zebra mussel invasion changes the kind and number of water plants present and decreases the amount and variety of fish.

Several programs around the state work to reduce the number of mussels. Illinois's state government instructs boat owners how to check their boats. Local governments and property owners use chemicals in the water as well as hot water to flush out the mussels. After fifteen years of zebra mussels, the fear of takeover has lessened. The real concern now is the spread of mussels into other waterways. Already they inhabit the Mississippi River and waterways in Wisconsin and Indiana.

Besides mussels, pollution from industry and from overuse has threatened other major state waterways. In 2003 the Illinois EPA funded local groups to study cleanup possibilities for five lakes in Jackson, Marion, Cook, Coles, and Vermilion counties. "The Illinois EPA takes pride in being able to partner with local groups and agencies to see [our lakes] are protected and improved for continuing use both for recreation and as wholesome sources of drinking water," said Renee Cipriano.

PROTECTING ENDANGERED SPECIES

Like many states, Illinois works to save wildlife whose populations have dipped dangerously low. Some species are under threat of disappearing completely. Every five years, a special panel evaluates and revises the list of endangered and threatened plants and animals found in Illinois. Some are on the federal endangered species list as well. In 1999 the Illinois list included 478 plant and animal groups. Once the list has been updated, the panel recommends ways to protect the threatened species and their habitats.

Once almost gone from the state, bobcats can now be found in most Illinois counties.

Once almost gone from Illinois, the bobcat was removed from the list in 1999. The panel found through an extensive statewide search that, between 1982 and 1998, these furry mammals were seen in 99 of 102 Illinois counties. To make sure the animal does not end up on the threatened list again, Southern Illinois University staff and graduate students attached radio collars to several bobcats in order to track and study their movements.

The state used a different approach with endangered river otters. First, state biologists studied the most favorable places for otters to thrive. Then they brought wild river otters from Louisiana and released them in the targeted watersheds. By 1997 more than three hundred otters had settled into their new homes across the state.

"Now river otters are so plentiful they are a problem to farm ponds because they eat so much fish," state biologist Joe Kath reports.

Kath's proudest success has been with the Indiana bat, which is found in Illinois and is on the federal endangered list. In the 1960s, scientists predicted that the worldwide population could be gone by 2010. To prevent this, Illinois environmental workers found and protected caves where the mammals hibernate, or spend the winter. "Although Indiana bat numbers are still declining everywhere else, Illinois has steadily increased its population," Kath says.

SEASONS COME AND GO

"I don't like the weather here," admits a Chicago-born businesswoman. "I'm not crazy about the hot summers and cold winters."

Many people dislike Illinois weather. Summers average 77 degrees Fahrenheit throughout the state. But the temperature can climb much higher and for several days in a row farther to the south. In 1988 Illinoisans suffered forty-seven days of summer heat above 90 degrees. The highest recorded temperature was 117 degrees in East Saint Louis on July 14, 1954.

The air tends to be humid along the state's many waterways. From July 12 to July 16 in 1995, for example, Chicago logged five brutal days of heat between 98 degrees and 104 degrees. High humidity made the heat feel even worse. The city suffered more than six hundred heat-related deaths during that time, more than any other midwestern state.

This girl enjoys the winter season by catching snowflakes on her tongue.

Winters are equally harsh. Temperatures can stay below freezing for weeks at a time. Illinois's average winter temperature is 30 degrees, but it drops lower farther north. The coldest temperature in the state was recorded on January 5, 1999. On that day, Congerville endured a chilling -36 degrees.

In winter, fast-moving snowstorms can appear without warning. Chicago baseball fans know that spring and fall games can end abruptly due to unexpected snowstorms. Large cities stockpile salt for sudden snow and ice that can cripple traffic and bury whole neighborhoods.

Land and Water

Galena
▲ Charles Mound (1,235 ft)
Rockford
Lake Michigan
Arlington Hts.
Chicago
Elgin
Batavia
Aurora
Naperville
Joliet
Hennepin Canal
Moline
Galesburg
Mississippi R.
Peoria
Illinois R.
Bloomington
Sangamon R.
Danville
Champaign
Quincy
Springfield
Decatur
New Salem
Kaskaskia R.
Effingham
Little Wabash R.
Wabash R.
Carlyle Lake
East St. Louis
Mt. Vernon
Mississippi R.
Carbondale
Ohio R.

Still, many Illinoisans prefer these extremes. "I like the four seasons," says senior citizen Gen Worshill. "I love autumn and spring. And winter holidays wouldn't be the same without snow."

Spring and summer breezes are often delightful in Illinois. Yet gentle winds can pick up speed across the plains and bring wild shifts in weather any time of year. Moist blasts of air can also whip from the waterways. Early Chicagoans described Lake Michigan winds "as strong enough to strip the fur off a buffalo."

Sometimes sharp winds can become quite extreme. Thunderstorms and tornadoes pound cities and farms with strong winds, sleet, and hail. Illinois averages twenty-six tornadoes each year. Many lose their force over the flatland or waterways. Others leave paths of death and destruction.

During July 1993, sheets of blinding rain fell over the Midwest. Rock Island reported 1.75 inches in only twenty minutes, a huge amount. The endless rain caused massive flooding in most rivers, especially the Mississippi. About 30,000 people fled their homes and businesses. More than 10,000 acres of farmland were soaked with the excess water, which cost billions of dollars in crop damage. Flooding renews the soil. But when it ruins crops, destroys homes, and forces people from their communities, it can do more harm than good.

The area around Prairie du Rocher, Illinois's oldest surviving town, was hit especially hard. Fifteen feet of water overflowed the two high stone levees along the Mississippi River, flooding the lowland farms leading into town. "Nobody had ever been through a natural disaster like that," agreed Debra and Jerry Burchell. "We rescued only a few goods from our shop at historic Fort de Chartres."

Still, local residents were encouraged by the show of support during this crisis. About 6,500 members of the National Guard arrived to remove residents and belongings. Volunteers rushed in from across the state to help.

Cornfields are a common sight in Illinois. Miles of them cover the state's flat countryside.

"My mom, younger brother, and I rode about three hours to a small town near Springfield," remembers fourteen-year-old Katie from Wilmette. "We shoveled sand into burlap bags. Other volunteers tied the bags and drove them in trucks to the river. People were really friendly." Together, Illinoisans can weather any storm—even horrendous floods and tornadoes.

Chapter Two

Illinois in the Making

The earliest known people to live in the future state of Illinois arrived more than ten thousand years ago. They lived together in small bands, fishing from the rivers and hunting animals for food and clothing. They also created simple tools from stone. But these native peoples did not generally stay in one place for long. They moved often to gather plants and track large animals. Many found shelter under limestone bluffs in what became southern Illinois.

Those who came after them stayed to build a new world. From about 1000 B.C.E. to 1600 C.E., woodland Indians farmed squash, pumpkin, and other seed-bearing plants. They made pottery for cooking and storing food. They buried their dead in earth mounds. Future generations called them Mound Builders.

MOUND BUILDERS

Waves of Mound Builders arrived in the state over a period of about 1,100 years. The Hopewell people established a network of trade routes that stretched from the Great Lakes to the Gulf of Mexico. Later the people now called American Indians brought corn from Mexico, copper

This 1735 illustration by Alexandre de Batz shows several Illinois Indians gathered in a clearing.

from Lake Superior, and shells from the Florida region. They made bows and arrows and flint hoes for tilling the soil.

Major cities developed along the Mississippi River between 500 and 1500 C.E. The largest prehistoric site north of Mexico is found at Cahokia near present-day Collinsville. At its peak, in 1050, as many as 30,000 people lived in the city. A chief and several priests ruled from the tops of massive platform mounds built in their honor. Cahokia boasted the tallest structure in North America until 1867. The people measured seasons, the time of day, and the stars with tall wooden poles. Archaeologists named their grouping of sun calendars Woodhenge because they resemble Stonehenge in England, another place where ancient people observed the heavens.

Between 1050 and 1150, Cahokia grew to become one of the largest urban centers in the world. The city's grass huts spread over nearly 6 square miles. As many as four thousand people crowded into each square mile, which is comparable to the population density of many major American cities today.

Starting in the 1200s, the number of Mound Builders slowly decreased. Some blame poor food, disease, or overcrowding for their disappearance. No one knows for sure. Visitors to the remaining mounds can only marvel at the sight of the once grand city and wonder.

THE ILLINIWEK

The Illiniwek, meaning "the people," were next to live in Illinois country. They thrived, planting corn and hunting buffalo. Their nation included the Cahokia, Peoria, Michigamea, Moingwena, and Tamaroa. These Algonquian-speaking tribes formed the largest family of Native Americans in the region.

In the early 1600s, warring Iroquois from the east moved into the Midwest. They were searching for new places to gather furs far away from European settlers. The Iroquois forced the Sauk and Fox into Illinois, where the Rock and Mississippi rivers joined.

American artist George Catlin created these illustrations of various Illiniwek Indians in the mid-1800s.

European explorers were not far behind. The first whites to explore Illiniwek country were French-Canadian Louis Jolliet and missionary Father Jacques Marquette. They reached the mouth of the Mississippi River on June 25, 1673.

Father Marquette wrote of a friendly meeting with the Indians: ". . . in token of peace, they presented their pipes to smoke. They then invited us to their village where all the tribe awaited us . . ."

For the next ninety years, the French claimed the Illinois Valley as their own. They spelled Illiniwek as Illinois, and gave the name to the river where most of the Illiniwek lived. Later Illinois became the state's official name.

Accounts of peaceful Indians and good hunting attracted fur traders. More priests came to convert the Indians to Christianity. The priests established the state's first permanent settlement near Cahokia.

In southern Illinois, the rich salt deposits that drew large buffalo herds and other animals brought white settlers as well. Charles de Saint Denis built a village and tannery near the Ohio River. He and his crew killed nearly 13,000 bison, or buffaloes, and sold their hides and tongues. Angered by their greed and waste, local Indians murdered the tannery workers. Few bison herds have roamed southern Illinois ever since.

The French built three main forts and several smaller ones in Illinois. Fort de Chartres and Fort Kaskaskia were government and military centers for the entire French-run Northwest Territory. Kaskaskia became a large village. Later, Fort de Chartres was rebuilt on its original foundation in western Illinois. Each year, locals gather in pioneer dress to remember the first French residents in Illinois country.

By the 1750s, the British demanded their share of the booming fur trade. They wanted control of all the territory inland from their eastern colonies. Tensions mounted, and soon French and British soldiers battled in what became known as the French and Indian War.

Indians joined the fight with France. They feared losing everything, as eastern Native Americans had, if the British invaded their land. By 1700 these worries grew as the Potawatomi moved south from lower Michigan to resettle in small villages near southern Lake Michigan and along northern Illinois rivers. They built wigwams of saplings covered with tree bark. The women planted corn and gathered wild fruits, while the men fished and hunted. The Potawatomi seemed well established. They would not leave their new homes without a fight.

But the French lost the war, and Kaskaskia fell into British hands. In 1763 France surrendered the entire Northwest Territory to the British. By 1800 many Potawatomi and other native nations were forced once again to move, this time west of the Mississippi River. Within forty years, most Indians had left Illinois.

STATEHOOD

A series of treaties with Indians opened yet more of their land to settlers. Pioneers swarmed into Illinois and pushed farther west. Steamboats aided the migration, greatly reducing travel time. Pioneers eyed Illinois country for its "soil 10 feet deep . . . fine as buckwheat flour . . . black as gunpowder." Soon farms and small towns cropped up across the Illinois countryside.

New settlers pressed for joining the young United States. On December 3, 1818, Illinois became the twenty-first state, with Kaskaskia as its capital. With only 35,000 people, Illinois had the smallest population of any state admitted to the Union. Yet, it became the doorway to the nation's spirited westward frontier.

The Peoria Indians paddled their canoes along the waterways of Illinois to trade with other native nations.

STATE FAIR

Where can you find a rodeo, carnival rides, pig races, funny-faced vegetables, and a huge cow carved in butter? At the Illinois state fair. Each summer it displays the best farm and homemade products the state has to offer, in addition to plenty of other attractions. In 1855 there was even a balloon. But the rope broke, and two kids went for an overnight ride. After they landed safely, ballooning ended at fairs.

"Illinois's state fairs began in 1853 to bring farmers together," says fair historian Patricia Henry. "That way, isolated farmers could meet and benefit from learning and competing with each other."

Fairs were so popular that local counties created their own. But the state fair in Springfield is the king of fairs. Almost half a million people come to its 366-acre fairground each year. Every fair opens with a parade and ribbon-cutting ceremony by the governor. Then the fun begins!

Settlers poured into Illinois, seeking land and fertile soil for farming.

Most people clustered in southern Illinois and along the rivers to the west. To coax settlers northward, Congress awarded each soldier from the French and Indian War 160 acres of land between the Illinois and Mississippi rivers. Within ten years, the state was overrun with new faces. By 1830 Illinois's population had grown to 150,000.

Grand Detour blacksmith John Deere helped this sudden growth along. Deere hated to stop every few feet to scrape clumps of Illinois soil from his iron plow blades, so he invented a steel plow blade that cut through the difficult soil. His invention made farming in Illinois much easier. Settlers arrived in even greater numbers to till and tame the land.

As new towns exploded with people, the state capital moved two more times. By 1839 lawmakers resettled in Springfield, where they stayed.

BLACK HAWK WAR

Pioneers drove many Indians into areas where it was often difficult to find enough food. In 1832 Chief Black Hawk led 1,500 Sauk back into Illinois to reclaim their cornfields.

"My reason teaches me that land cannot be sold," wrote sixty-four-year-old Black Hawk. "The Great Spirit gave it to his children to live upon. So long as they occupy and cultivate it, they have a right to the soil."

Settlers disagreed. Fierce fighting broke out in what became known as the Black Hawk War. During four months of clashes, more than one

Black Hawk was an important Sauk leader who battled the settlers taking over Indian lands.

thousand Indian men, women, and children died. In the end, Native Americans lost even more of their homeland. The Black Hawk War marked "the last Indian war fought east of the Mississippi River."

A LAND DIVIDED

From the beginning, the state was deeply divided over the question of slavery. At the time Illinois joined the Union, four of every six Illinois residents came from the South. Unlike Northerners, most Southerners insisted that they needed slaves to tend their fields. Many brought their ideas and their slaves with them when they moved to Illinois.

The Illinois constitution forbade slavery. Yet the government allowed John Crenshaw to lease hundreds of slaves from their owners in the slave state of Kentucky. Crenshaw's salt-making business prospered from the government-owned wells in Shawneetown. Its profits supplied 14 percent of Illinois's annual income. So state lawmakers let Crenshaw run his 30,000-acre estate as "a slave state within a free state." Terrible rumors spread through town about how Crenshaw kidnapped hundreds of free blacks and runaway slaves. People said he held them in chains on his mansion's third floor. Then he put them to work or sold them into slavery in the South.

During the 1830s and 1840s, many easterners and overseas immigrants arrived in northern and central Illinois. The Illinois and Michigan Canal (I&M) helped open the region to the Industrial Age. Newcomers built roads, mined coal, and manufactured goods. Many never understood how one person could own another. They pushed to end slavery in Illinois and throughout the nation.

Abraham Lincoln, a self-taught Springfield lawyer, tried to understand both sides. Finally, he reasoned that "although volume upon volume is written to prove slavery a very good thing, we never hear of the man who wishes to take the good of it by being a slave himself."

Groups for and against slavery organized around the state. Secret societies such as the proslavery Knights of the Golden Circle plotted to help slave owners. A mob killed Elijah Lovejoy of Alton for his writings, which called for the end of slavery.

On the opposing front, women formed the Illinois Antislavery Society for Women. Free blacks worked with schools and churches to end local laws that favored catching runaway slaves. Illinois became an important path along the Underground Railroad, the secret route to freedom for runaways.

In 1858 six-foot four-inch Abraham Lincoln ran against five-foot four-inch Stephen Douglas for U.S. senator. Douglas, nicknamed the Little Giant, wanted to build a railroad running the length of the state. He hoped to aid growth in the state and to link Southern businesses with Great Lakes shipping routes. Once the new railroad had been built, many central Illinois towns sprang up around key stops along its route.

Abraham Lincoln (standing, center) was known for his way with words and his ability to deliver powerful, often stirring speeches. He entered into a series of debates with Stephen Douglas (seated to Lincoln's right) in 1858, as both men vied for a seat in the U.S. Senate.

Lincoln and Douglas disagreed about slavery. They aired their views in a series of debates that took place across Illinois. Lincoln upheld the view he had given voice to for decades, "The institution of slavery is founded on both injustice and bad policy." But he was unable to get the support of enough voters. He lost the election but brought greater attention to Illinois and to himself as a great speaker against slavery. In 1860 Lincoln was elected the sixteenth president of the United States.

Soon after his election, the country erupted into civil war. Whole towns of men formed regiments to fight on behalf of the North. Many boys, such as Orion (aged twelve) and Lyston (aged nine) Howe of Waukegan, enlisted as drummer boys. Others refused to join the fight against slavery. Some Knights of the Golden Circle even pulled out their teeth rather than aid the Northern cause. Soldiers needed teeth to bite on cartridges before loading their guns.

Cairo, near the southern tip of Illinois, was alive with activity during the Civil War. Union soldiers left from the town to battle Southern forces to the west.

Illinoisans played a central role in the war. Almost 260,000 soldiers fought, and about 35,000 died in battle. To support the troops, Galesburg's George Brown invented a new machine that planted corn. The corn planter greatly increased the amount of food the Midwest could supply to Northern soldiers. Women formed aid societies to nurse sick soldiers and worked in factories and at the various other jobs left by men who went to fight. Factory towns became major suppliers of weapons.

One Illinois soldier who played a major role in the Civil War was Galena's General Ulysses S. Grant. Grant led troops to defeat General Robert E. Lee in the final battle of the war. After Lee surrendered, a thoughtful Grant told his troops, "The rebels are our Countrymen again." In 1868 Grant became the nation's eighteenth president, a post he held for two terms.

The war proved difficult for the nation. The person most credited with keeping the country together and ending slavery was Abraham Lincoln. Five days after the war officially ended, however, Lincoln was shot. The nation grieved as he was buried in a tomb in Springfield. In central Illinois, places important to his remarkable career became historic sites. Today, Illinoisans proudly call their state "the Land of Lincoln."

A HERO PASSES

Author Carl Sandburg was struck by how much the people loved General Grant. After Grant died in 1885, seven-year-old Sandburg watched Galesburg citizens—black and white—honor their hero.

I remember a couple of cannon came past with six or eight horses pulling them. The Negro Silver Cornet Band marched. They were the only black faces in the parade, and as they passed I saw faces of men and women light up . . . there was something people liked about seeing the black men playing sad music because General Grant, who had helped them get free, was dead.

The Chicago fire of September 15, 1859, burned for more than six hours, claiming five city blocks. An even greater blaze was to grip the city in 1871.

"CHICAGO SHALL RISE AGAIN"

Illinois thrived after the Civil War. State farmers raised the most corn and wheat in the nation. More miles of railroad tracks than in any other state linked farm towns with cities where crops were sold. Illinois had become the nation's breadbasket. Hogs and cows became big business in the state as well, especially in Chicago's stockyards.

Then, on October 8, 1871, disaster struck Chicago. At about 9:00 p.m., fire erupted in Kate and Patrick O'Leary's barn. Legend blames a cow for kicking over the lantern. But the exact cause of the fire remains unknown.

What followed were twenty-seven hours of terror. Thirty-mile-per-hour winds pushed the flames closer to the city's center. Wooden houses and stores quickly burned. Soon the extreme heat and sparks jumped the Chicago River. The fire raged out of control.

One observer wrote: "There was sudden screaming and dashing about of half-clad women, gathering up valuables . . . frantic rushing into the streets. . . . Everywhere dust, smoke, flame, heat, thunder of falling walls, crackle of fire, hissing of water, panting of engine, roar of wind, and uproar."

A light rain helped cool the last ashes. By then, nearly 20,000 buildings lay in ruin. About 300 people had died, and 104,500 were homeless.

Despite the setback, Chicago was rebuilt with amazing speed. New fire codes required steel and stone buildings, which resisted fire. *Chicago Daily* headlines declared, "Chicago Shall Rise Again."

Chicago healed in time to hold the 1893 World's Columbian Exposition. The city put on a grand show for the fair. Magnificent buildings, the first observation wheel, and art from around the world showcased the city and state.

Factories sprang up throughout Illinois. By 1900 Illinois had fourteen cities with more than 100,000 people. Chicago was the state's largest city, with almost 1.7 million residents. Waves of European immigrants and blacks from the South flooded into the city to work in food-processing plants, clothing factories, steel mills, and construction.

Wealthy business owners prospered in Chicago. But their workers suffered greatly. Most toiled at ten- to fourteen-hour workdays in filthy, unsafe conditions. At night they went home to overcrowded, run-down neighborhoods.

Several major labor protests began in Chicago. Workers organized to call for eight-hour workdays, increased wages, and laws against hiring children. Chicagoan Mary O'Reilly explains the struggle:

Just to labor for bread,
Just to work and be fed.
For this we have marched
Through the snow-covered street.

The Ferris wheel loomed large, towering high above Chicago's 1893 World's Columbian Exposition, a major international fair.

El-a-Noy

The unknown poet who wrote the flowery words to "El-a-noy" was inspired by the biblical King Solomon and the Queen of Sheba as well as by the twelfth-century French philosopher Peter Abelard and the great love of his life, the fair Heloise.

Chorus

Then move your fam-'ly west-ward, Good health you will en-joy, And rise to wealth and hon-or in the State of El - a - noy.

'Twas here the Queen of Sheba came,
With Solomon of old,
With an ass-load of spices,
Pomegranates and gold;
And when she saw this lovely land,
Her heart was filled with joy,
Straightway she said: "I'd like to be
A Queen of El-a-noy." *Chorus*

Away up in the northward,
Right on the border line,
A great commercial city,
Chicago, you will find.
Her men are all like Abelard,
Her women like Heloise;
All honest virtuous people,
For they live in El-a-noy. *Chorus*

She's bounded by the Wabash,
The Ohio and the Lakes,
She's crawfish in the swampy lands,
The mild-sick and the shakes;
But these are slight diversions
And take not from the joy
Of living in this garden land,
The State of El-a-noy. *Chorus*

On May 4, 1886, a bomb exploded at a peaceful Chicago worker rally in Haymarket Square. Police panicked, and violence exploded. After a flurry of gunfire, seven policemen and two onlookers lay dead.

The police arrested eight labor leaders for causing the riot. After an unfair trial, four were hanged, and one committed suicide. Later, the governor cleared the others.

A statue in front of the police department training center honors the officers who died. At first, to recall their dead friends, Chicago workers observed special May Day celebrations. Then the idea of honoring workers spread to other nations as well. Today, the day that began to remember hardworking Chicagoans is also celebrated in eastern Europe and Russia.

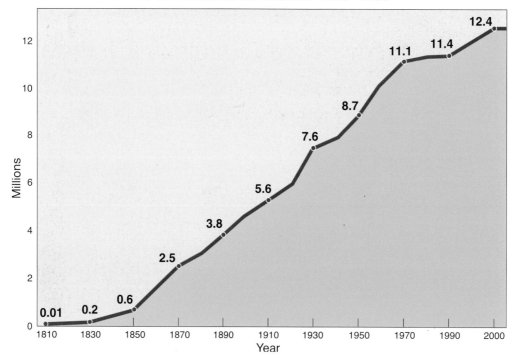

POPULATION GROWTH: 1810–2000

Jane Addams of Cedarville started the settlement house movement in the United States to ease problems of the poor. She opened Hull House in Chicago as a safe place within a slum. Hull House helped immigrants find medical care, education, work, and food. The settlement house provided children with kindergarten classes and after-school clubs. Addams published papers documenting the terrible conditions that existed in the surrounding neighborhood. She also fought for better jobs, schools, housing, garbage collection, and health care. Her fight spurred the nation to improve the lives of the poor.

Jane Addams holds a little girl at an event marking the fortieth anniversary of Hull House, a center she set up to aid poor families.

Given its experience facing tough social problems, Illinois led the country on many public issues. In 1891 the state was the first to pass child labor laws and create separate courts for children. Illinois provided wages to sick workers and passed the first "mother's aid" law, granting money for the care of helpless children.

The boldest move, however, came in 1913. Illinois was the first state east of the Mississippi River to allow women to vote. Strong women, such as Jane Addams and Myra Bradwell, the state's first female lawyer, pushed for women's rights at home and in the workplace. Bradwell fought so Illinois women could keep their own wages and care for their children after divorce. Many women claim that Bradwell "probably changed the course of women's legal rights."

ILLINOIS TODAY

Into the twentieth century, Illinois continued to lead the country in farming, industry, and transportation. The state played a major role during World Wars I and II. Factories in Chicago, Rockford, Peoria, and Rantoul worked overtime to make weapons, tanks, and planes. Weapons storehouses cropped up in Joliet and Rantoul. Once again, farmers shipped foods to war-torn areas to feed the soldiers.

On December 2, 1942, University of Chicago's Enrico Fermi and a team of scientists set off the first nuclear chain reaction. This experiment led to the first atomic bomb, which helped end World War II. Moreover, Fermi's discovery ushered our nation and the world into the atomic age.

The country's postwar boom made the state's economy even stronger. Factories turned to making profitable peacetime goods. Argonne National Laboratory near Chicago opened an atomic research center. Fermi Laboratory in Batavia created the world's most powerful atom smasher. By 1960 Illinois was the country's largest steel producer and a leader in computer and atomic energy research.

Chicago quickly became a melting pot. In this photograph from the mid-1930s, a vendor sells goods from his pushcart in the heart of the city's Greek neighborhood.

But the population and business changes that troubled the nation during the 1970s and 1980s eventually affected Illinois as well. Interstate highways cut through farmlands. Motels and shopping malls opened near exits. Shoppers preferred to drive to the outskirts of town for their goods, leaving city centers to decay.

Prices for farm products dropped, causing profits to decline. Many farmers sold their land and found other better-paying jobs. Urban factories moved to suburbs or to other states altogether. Some produced goods overseas where costs were cheaper.

The residents of Chicago's many neighborhoods take pride in their city. Through improvement projects, they put a bright face on the future of the state's largest urban center.

Without industry taxes to pay for services, cities and towns suffered. Poor schools, increased crime, and run-down housing doomed many neighborhoods. Those who could afford to move headed to the suburbs or followed jobs out of the state.

Others gave up on city life and left for smaller towns. Debbie Brooks quit a good chemist's job to live in Chester, an Illinois town of about eight thousand people. "I like little towns like this," she said. "The quality of life is better, and there's less crime than in a big city."

Life for Illinoisans improved during the 1990s. The state and national governments focused their spending on rebuilding cities. New industries, such as aerospace companies, moved to Illinois. The economy boomed, and as a result the state raised more money from taxes. Government officials used the money to build and improve roads and to continue sprucing up urban areas across the state.

The new prosperity brought some major changes to Illinois. Despite population shifts to suburbs and smaller towns, the state's cities found their numbers staying the same. This was because people from around the world continued to flock to Illinois. Hispanics and Asians in particular have added to the changing face of Illinois. Their presence and influence can be felt across the state. Just like the first settlers, they come in search of a better life.

In the twenty-first century, like the rest of the country, the state economy has taken a turn for the worse. People are out of work, and many businesses are closing. The state struggles to improve life for its growing population. Still, through it all, Illinoisans are working hard to make their families, communities, and state as strong and successful as they can be.

Chapter Three

Everyday Illinoisans

"It's bad luck to step over a broom," warned Abe Lincoln's Irish-English father. "An itchy nose means you'll kiss a fool," reminds a grandmother of Russian ancestry. "If you toss your shoe in the air and it lands standing up, you will have good luck that day," explains a Wilmette woman born in Tokyo, Japan.

Unusual sayings color almost everyone's childhood in Illinois. With the sayings come varied customs, religions, and foods. Many of these customs are brought by recent immigrants to Illinois. Others have been passed down through families that have lived in the state for many generations.

POPULATIONS THROUGHOUT THE STATE

With 12.6 million people in 2002, Illinois has the sixth-largest population in the United States. Eighty-five percent of these people live in or near cities. Most reside in Chicago and its surrounding areas. Crowded city neighborhoods mean more people compete for houses and jobs.

These Illinoisans are treated to the heart-stopping twists and turns of a roller coaster at one of the state's amusement parks.

A recently married couple celebrates in Beardstown. The state's plentiful jobs have drawn many new residents from Mexico as well as from around the world.

Illinois's population is moving in two directions. One trend points toward whites leaving the state in greater numbers while growing populations of Hispanic and Asian Americans replace them. Recent studies reveal that the Hispanic population is expected to grow by 30 percent and the Asian population by almost 20 percent. These increases seem huge when compared to the less than 5 percent growth rates for the state's black and white populations.

The other trend involves a massive push outward from Chicago's city limits. The suburbs have been the site of some of the state's major growth.

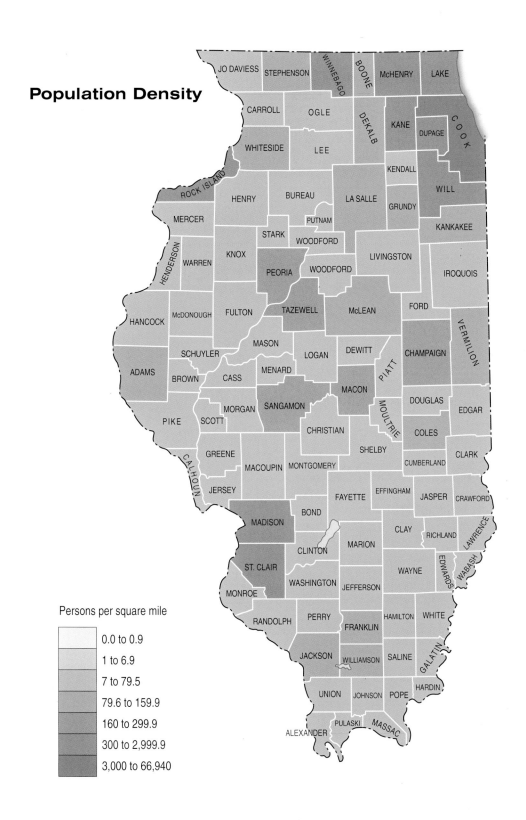

Population Density

Persons per square mile

- 0.0 to 0.9
- 1 to 6.9
- 7 to 79.5
- 79.6 to 159.9
- 160 to 299.9
- 300 to 2,999.9
- 3,000 to 66,940

JO DAVIESS, STEPHENSON, WINNEBAGO, BOONE, McHENRY, LAKE, CARROLL, OGLE, DEKALB, KANE, DUPAGE, COOK, WHITESIDE, LEE, KENDALL, WILL, ROCK ISLAND, HENRY, BUREAU, LA SALLE, GRUNDY, MERCER, PUTNAM, KANKAKEE, STARK, WOODFORD, HENDERSON, WARREN, KNOX, PEORIA, WOODFORD, LIVINGSTON, IROQUOIS, McDONOUGH, FULTON, TAZEWELL, McLEAN, FORD, HANCOCK, VERMILION, MASON, LOGAN, DEWITT, CHAMPAIGN, SCHUYLER, ADAMS, BROWN, CASS, MENARD, MACON, PIATT, DOUGLAS, EDGAR, MORGAN, SANGAMON, MOULTRIE, COLES, PIKE, SCOTT, CHRISTIAN, SHELBY, CLARK, GREENE, MACOUPIN, MONTGOMERY, CUMBERLAND, JERSEY, FAYETTE, EFFINGHAM, JASPER, CRAWFORD, CALHOUN, MADISON, BOND, CLAY, RICHLAND, LAWRENCE, CLINTON, MARION, WAYNE, EDWARDS, WABASH, ST. CLAIR, WASHINGTON, JEFFERSON, MONROE, RANDOLPH, PERRY, FRANKLIN, HAMILTON, WHITE, JACKSON, WILLIAMSON, SALINE, GALATIN, UNION, JOHNSON, POPE, HARDIN, ALEXANDER, PULASKI, MASSAC

Still Chicago remains one of the few major cities to gain population in recent years. This change, too, results largely from the arrival of Mexican and other international migrants. By 2000 census figures showed that Cook County, which contains Chicago, added 50,000 new residents. This number offsets the 97,000 who left the city limits but stayed nearby.

"Chicago has had a long history of immigrant waves replacing immigrants waves," says Abel Nunez, head of the Chicago social service agency Centro Romero.

The search for cheaper, safer housing has driven many people farther from the city. In 1950 Chicago's population reached a peak at 3.6 million residents. In 2000 Chicago's population had fallen to 2.9 million. Chicago and its surrounding areas currently make up 44 percent of the state's population. Now more Illinois kids live in suburbs, rather than in the city or on farms, than ever before.

Illinois continues to attract greater numbers of immigrants than any midwestern state. Changes in Latin America and Asia spur some immigrants to seek a new life in America. Most Illinois immigrants come to Chicago for the greater number and variety of jobs the city offers. As a result, Chicago has the greatest ethnic diversity of any American city outside of New York City and Washington, D.C. Hispanic residents total more than 12 percent of the state population and 26 percent of Chicago's. Another 10 percent come from Poland. They form the largest Polish community outside of Poland. And there is a large Japanese-American community that has lived in the state for decades. Many moved from California after the outbreak of World War II.

Newcomers represent nearly every country of the world. Restaurants offer everything from sweet Thai noodles and sushi to homemade tortillas. Students in one North Side Chicago school speak thirty-five different languages, including Urdu, Mayan, and Vietnamese. The difficulty for many schools is finding teachers who can talk to children in their native language while helping them adjust to life in America.

"Here kids are taught fifty-fifty in their language and English in our school. After three years, they are thrown to the wolves, totally in English-speaking classes," says teacher Lucy Klocksin.

So many Indian- and Pakistani-owned stores line West Devon Avenue that the area is called the Sari Capital of the Midwest. Many south Asian women travel hundreds of miles to buy material for their traditional outfits. One stretch of the street has been renamed Gandhi Marg after the famous Indian leader and activist.

A Chicago shopkeeper pauses from his work selling Chinese herbs and medicines.

The next mile is Golda Meir Boulevard. This section honors the Russian-born American who became Israel's beloved prime minister from 1969 to 1974. Her name on street signs reflects the neighborhood's Israeli and Jewish populations.

Cities and towns throughout Illinois celebrate their ethnic roots. Many were named by their original settlers. Moline, meaning "milltown" in French, has one of the largest Belgian communities outside of Belgium. In 1907 the city claimed the first newspaper in the United States written in Flemish. Today Moline is a melting pot of Belgians, Greeks, African Americans, and Mexican Americans.

ETHNIC ILLINOIS

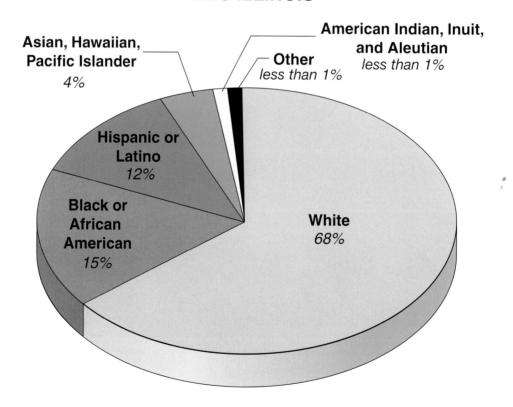

Asian, Hawaiian, Pacific Islander 4%

American Indian, Inuit, and Aleutian less than 1%

Other less than 1%

Hispanic or Latino 12%

Black or African American 15%

White 68%

BLACK COMMUNITIES

About 15 percent of Illinoisans and 37 percent of Chicagoans are African American. This group, more than others, has faced many racial barriers through the years. Yet African Americans have played an important role in the state's progress.

Haitian-born Jean Baptiste Point du Sable was Illinois's first permanent non-Native American settler. In about 1779 he and his Potawatomi wife, Catherine, built a thriving trade center on what is now Chicago's elegant Michigan Avenue. Twenty years later, he moved his family to East Peoria where they lived with the Potawatomi.

Runaway slaves trickled into Illinois during the early 1800s and settled near key points along the Underground Railroad. After the Civil War ended in 1865, even larger numbers of freed blacks arrived. Most settled along major railway routes, forming communities in Jacksonville, Champaign, Galesburg, and Chicago.

George W. Smith, an escaped slave, was one of the first successful black landowners in Illinois. He saved to buy 80 acres of land in 1876. By 1900 he owned 437 acres in Champaign County. His youngest son, John Smith, expanded the farm to include 600 acres. John died in 1968. The surviving family members have kept the farm as a memorial to their ancestors who struggled so hard to succeed.

World Wars I and II triggered large black migrations northward to fill wartime job openings and find greater freedom. Busloads of blacks left poor farms in Kentucky for the northern "promised land." Crossing the border into Cairo, Illinois, caused the greatest thrill.

According to the major Chicago newspaper the *Tribune*, "There black passengers did something they never would have dreamed of doing in the South. They moved to seats at the front of the bus." In Kentucky they would have been jailed or beaten for sitting there.

By 1918, 60,000 blacks lived in Chicago. Poet Carl Sandburg reported, "Every time a lynching takes place in a community down south . . . people from that community will arrive in Chicago inside of two weeks."

Many reached fame never dreamed of in the South. Adelbert Roberts became the first black state senator in 1924. Bessie Coleman was the first woman and black to earn a pilot's license. The highway leading to Chicago's O'Hare Airport honors her triumphs.

Yet African Americans never fully escaped racial hatred in the North. Unwritten social laws limited most blacks to cramped neighborhoods and low-paying jobs as railroad porters, maids, and day workers. In Chicago, real estate brokers rented to blacks only in a South Side area that became known as Bronzeville because of its overcrowded, all-black population.

In the mid-1930s, many of the businesses in south Chicago's Bronzeville neighborhood were owned or operated by black residents.

This six-year-old wears a kinta cloth hat that recalls his African roots.

Angry blacks worked to change these disturbing trends. They pushed for better jobs, schools, and housing, and for an end to police cruelty. Widespread tensions between whites and African Americans erupted in East Saint Louis in 1917. A white mob swept through the city, burning 240 black-owned buildings and killing fifty people. Within two years, the madness had spread to Chicago.

Rock-throwing whites killed a black boy who swam past an unofficial line separating the black beach from the ones used by whites. Violence exploded after police refused to arrest the killers. Three days of rage left twenty blacks and fourteen whites dead, more than one hundred injured, and scores of black homes burned.

Despite these challenges and setbacks, the state's black community grew and prospered. Chicago's black population rose from 492,000 to one million between 1950 and 1970. The South Side became known as the black capital of America. Black culture flowered as world-famous musicians, writers, and artists got their start there.

In 1968 riots erupted once again after Martin Luther King Jr., the famous African-American civil rights leader, was shot. In Chicago, black mobs ran through the streets, burning entire neighborhoods. Anger and protest flared again in the 1980s. Poor blacks felt abandoned by state and federal governments. Severe budget cuts limited programs for better jobs, schools, and homes. Many hopeless youths turned to drugs and the violence it often brings.

Today, violence in some neighborhoods is so widespread that kids fear walking to school or playgrounds. Parents in Chicago housing projects worry their kids won't live to see another birthday. One mother pays eighty dollars per month for burial insurance for her five children, who are under thirteen years of age.

Still, a generation of successful blacks has come from years of racial conflict in Illinois. Their ranks include many celebrated artists, such as blues singer Muddy Waters, as well as former U.S. senator Jesse Jackson Jr., Mae Jemison (the first black woman astronaut), two-time Olympic track star Jackie Joyner-Kersee, and John Harold Johnson, a leading Chicago businessman. One of the most well-known Chicagoans is Oprah Winfrey. She is a respected actress, talk-show host, owner of media businesses, and one of the richest people in the United States.

RELIGIONS

Illinoisans practice a range of religions that mirror their varied origins. A large number of people throughout the state are Christians, mainly Roman Catholic or members of different Protestant sects such as

Presbyterian, Baptist, Methodist, and Lutheran. Larger cities support Jewish synagogues, Greek Orthodox churches, Buddhist shrines, and Muslim mosques.

Wilmette is home to the awesome Bahá'í House of Worship. The Bahá'í religion was founded in Persia, now Iran, more than one hundred years ago. The Bahá'ís chose Wilmette as the center of their North American movement. Wilmette's grand lacy-domed building took forty years to complete. The white marble palace is one of only seven Bahá'í houses of worship worldwide.

The smaller religions of the Mennonites, Mormons (Church of Latter-day Saints), and Society of Friends have large followings in Illinois as well. In 1839 Mormon prophet Joseph Smith led followers to Nauvoo, which means "beautiful place" in Hebrew. He founded the town after prejudice and violence forced the Mormons out of Missouri. Nauvoo prospered so much that other settlers feared the growing Mormon power. They killed Smith and his brother and drove off the Mormons, this time to Utah.

These Muslim women have gathered on a bench at Chicago's Lincoln Park Zoo.

Today, the Reorganized Church of Latter-day Saints operates a visitor site that preserves the Mormon shrine. Each August, Mormons present the outdoor musical, *City of Joseph*. The people of Nauvoo also hold ceremonies on Labor Day to remember the waves of immigrants that grew grapes and made cheese, as their European ancestors had done.

For some communities, church activities guide every aspect of daily life. Amish live the same simple lifestyle as when they were driven from Switzerland during the mid-1800s. Work and prayer fill their days.

The Amish reject such modern developments as electricity, cars, and television. Instead, they travel by horse-drawn buggy, farm without power machines, and dress in plain, dark clothes. Most Amish children attend one-room schoolhouses.

Illinois is one of five states with active Amish settlements. The non-Amish residents of Arthur and Arcola respect Amish privacy and enjoy the products of Amish life. Stores carry Amish hand-carved furniture and needlework crafts. The Amish are also known for their cooking and baking. They sell white and fruit breads, pies, jams, and cheeses in their stores and restaurants.

SCHOOLS

Illinois schools offer a range of opportunities. The best schools are found in districts that can afford extra programs, higher teacher salaries, and up-to-date supplies. Wealthier districts are also able to send students on field trips, including the annual authors fair in Springfield, where the state honors hundreds of talented young writers from around Illinois.

The worst schools are often located in run-down city centers and in thinly populated rural areas. They lack funds for art, music, and physical education, key subjects that help offer a well-rounded educa-tion and that many students love. Teachers in poorer areas may receive few supplies, and kids learn from old textbooks.

WEDDING OF THE WINE AND CHEESE

Long ago in southern France, a shepherd boy forgot his lunch in a cave. Curds, lumps of thickened milk, and bread sat in the cool limestone cave for many months. When he returned, the boy discovered that the bread had become hard and uneatable. But surprisingly the curds were protected by tasty streaks of mold. The French who came to Nauvoo claim this was the beginning of blue cheese.

Nauvoo celebrates an annual grape festival the weekend before Labor Day. At the festival, actors stage a wedding between the bride of wine and the bridegroom of cheese. The marriage symbolizes how well this food and drink go together. A shepherd boy appears in the ceremony, leading the way to this perfect marriage of tastes.

The results of these problems can last a lifetime for many Illinois students. In some areas without enough money, four of every ten third graders cannot read at their grade level, and national test scores are low. The same ratio of students never finishes high school. That is an alarming number when compared to the average statewide dropout rate, which falls to five out of every 100 students.

Another key issue is testing. Each year, the state requires students in grades 3, 4, 5, 7, and 8 to take a test prepared by the state. Stakes are high in some districts. In Chicago, students who do not pass the test must go to summer school. If they cannot pass the test after summer school, they must repeat that grade. Several school districts also require students to take a national test. Many teachers are opposed to so much testing. They argue that tests and the class hours spent preparing for them take too much time away from more important subjects.

Safety is another problem in many Illinois schools. Some principals hire off-duty police officers as guards. They lock doors during school hours and use metal detectors to search kids for weapons. Several schools ban clothing or jewelry that may suggest gang membership. Some have eliminated time outdoors, such as for recess and after lunchtime.

"Our state and federal governments underfund schools," says an angry inner-city teacher. Illinois ranks forty-ninth out of the fifty states in providing its public schools with equal funding. To make matters worse, in 1999 legislators passed a bill allowing families to pay fewer taxes if they send their kids to nonpublic schools. This policy reduces the amount of money available for public schools and the quality teachers they need.

One in six Illinois families turn to nonpublic schools for their children. Illinois's largest private school system is run by the Roman Catholic Church. Even the church, however, closes schools in poorer neighborhoods when money is tight.

Two sixth graders share homework tips. Illinoisans are proud of their strong schools and their many hardworking students.

When the church threatened to close Providence Saint Mel, principal Paul Adams fought back. He ran a tough, but safe school for Chicago inner-city students. Adams became the school's devoted fund-raiser, teacher, bus driver, and gardener. When thieves broke in, he moved into the school as well.

Chicago's Oprah Winfrey celebrated Adams and his school in a television special. His greatest achievement is the overwhelming number of graduates—99 percent—from gang-infested neighborhoods who go on to college.

Under the watchful eye of the professor, students conduct an experiment as part of a cell biology class. The future is being shaped today at the state's many colleges and universities.

"We expect you to be the best and competitive," he tells new students. "We expect you to make this a better world. You are special."

Illinois's students choose from an outstanding network of colleges and universities in their state. The main campus of the University of Illinois in Champaign-Urbana brings together more than 38,000 students from 50 states and 100 nations. More than nine state-supported universities operate throughout Illinois, including a network of colleges and junior colleges in the Chicago area.

"Most people think Illinois is for farmers only," explains fund-raiser Judy Checker. "They aren't aware of the research firsts from here."

So many supercomputer advances were developed at the Urbana campus that east-central Illinois became known as the Silicon Prairie. In addition, the school was the first major university to provide programs for students with disabilities, including opportunities for Sharon Hedrick (gold in 1984 and 1988) and Jean Driscoll (silver in 1992) to win Special Olympic medals for wheelchair racing.

Illinois residents are proud of their private colleges, too. When Northwestern University's football team went to the Rose Bowl in 1996 for the first time in forty-seven years, all of Evanston went wild. Jacksonville residents quickly point out that MacMurray College offered the first advanced degrees to women in the nation. And nearby Illinois College, an important station along the Underground Railroad, teaches state-of-the-art methods for working with children who are deaf.

Equally impressive are the more than seventy-five Nobel Prize winners who attended or taught at the University of Chicago. On Chicago's North Side, Native American College, NACE (Native American Community for Education), is the only midwestern school devoted to preserving tribal culture. Through its many first-rate schools, Illinois offers its students the tools for a bright and successful future.

Chapter Four

Inside Government

"Illinois has many strengths," says state senator Jeffrey Schoenberg. "We just need to coordinate between the city of Chicago and the rest of the state." The state's leaders work hard to make sure the interests of all the state's regions are served.

THE ENGINE THAT RUNS THE STATE

Illinois government tries to balance the interests of all its citizens. More than four thousand workers carry out jobs for one of the three government branches: executive, legislative, and judicial.

Executive

Every four years, Illinois voters elect six officers to the executive branch. The governor serves as head of all executive departments and committees, just as the U.S. president does. Each governor prepares a yearly state budget, appoints hundreds of managers, approves or vetoes (rejects) bills and contracts, and oversees the state military.

Some governors aim to shake up more than their state government. In 1999 George Ryan became the first governor to visit Cuba since that nation became off-limits to U.S. visitors and businesses in 1962.

Visitors to central Illinois can take tours of the grand state capitol in Springfield.

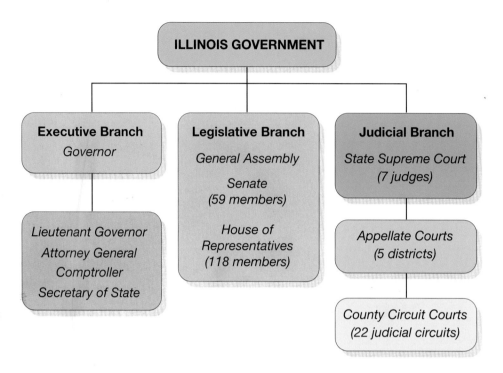

ILLINOIS GOVERNMENT

Executive Branch
Governor

*Lieutenant Governor
Attorney General
Comptroller
Secretary of State*

Legislative Branch

General Assembly

*Senate
(59 members)*

*House of
Representatives
(118 members)*

Judicial Branch

*State Supreme Court
(7 judges)*

*Appellate Courts
(5 districts)*

*County Circuit Courts
(22 judicial circuits)*

Ryan felt that the United States had punished Cuban citizens long enough for having a form of government U.S. leaders opposed. He also wanted new business opportunities for Illinoisans. No firm plans have been adopted yet, but the trip made many national government leaders talk about change.

Legislative

The Illinois legislature, called the General Assembly, includes 59 senators and 118 representatives. Voters select one representative from their district to serve a term of two years. Senators serve terms of either four years or two years.

The General Assembly creates or changes laws and approves the state budget. A majority of members in each house must approve of a bill for it to pass successfully. Then the governor signs it into law. If the governor vetoes the bill, it can still become law. But three-fifths of each house of the General Assembly must still be in support of it.

Much like the federal government, Illinois runs according to a constitution. This body of rules sets up how the state government conducts its business. It also outlines the rights that are granted to all citizens. Items in the constitution can be amended, or changed, by legislators, but most wait until the entire document is updated and revised. Legislators voted on the last rewrite of the constitution on December 15, 1970.

Judicial

The judicial branch includes more than 400 elected judges and the 350 associate judges they appoint. Their job is to translate the state constitution into law.

Most people involved in a court case appear before one of Illinois's twenty-two circuit courts. Those unhappy with a ruling can appear before an appellate court or the supreme court, the state's highest judicial body. Cook County, which includes Chicago, has one of the largest court systems in the country. But even with more than four hundred judges, people often wait months for their hearing.

TIPPING THE BALANCE

On January 31, 2000, Governor George Ryan took another brave stand. This one shook judicial systems across the country. Two weeks earlier, the Illinois supreme court had cleared a man of the charges that had placed him on death row. Because this was the thirteenth similar case in Illinois, Ryan halted the state's policy of sentencing some criminals to die. He said courts were unfair to minorities, who often had fewer good lawyers to help them. Until the system changed, he refused to put criminals to death.

Before he left office in 2003, Ryan released thirteen more wrongfully convicted men and changed the sentences of all prisoners in Illinois awaiting execution. Courts everywhere took notice. Many people who were polled agreed with the governor's action. Newspapers around the country covered the men's release. Most European countries do not have the death penalty, so many of their leaders sent messages of support. Since then, the issue has not gone away. But Ryan's bold move has reopened a national debate on this life-and-death issue.

THE CHICAGO MACHINE AND DOWNSTATE

Illinois divides into more bodies of local government than any other state. This confusing assortment of agencies often overlaps and competes for money and power. Some of the state's biggest struggles are between Chicago and the rest of the state.

Chicago's former mayor Richard J. Daley, father of current mayor Richard M. Daley, built a powerful city "machine" between 1955 and 1976. His idea of government was to trade favors, such as granting jobs in exchange for votes. Many voters did what they were told to get the extra perks from lawmakers, so the mayor often got the support he needed. Citizens who didn't go along often received terrible threats, city workers would say. "Don't vote [my way] and you lose your public housing or food checks."

Daley's Chicago became known as "the city that worked." Moreover, Daley's influence reached beyond Illinois into other state governments and national elections. Illinois earned a reputation as the Midwest president-maker because Daley could guarantee votes to national candidates. "What Daley needs, Daley gets," said one observer.

Daley's machine created great distrust, which continues to this day, among Illinois districts. Those outside the city believe Chicago politicians hold too much power, even though the city's population has declined and recent mayors have claimed far less power. Growing suburbs want their own needs met, such as expanding highways to meet increased traffic demands.

"Downstaters feel their concerns are better heard by a downstater as governor," admits former Rantoul mayor Katy Podagrosi.

Still, current Chicago mayor Richard M. Daley pushes programs that benefit the city, such as enlarging airports and creating more lakefront parks. In an unusual show of force, he secretly bulldozed a lakefront airport in the middle of the night. He said it was to protect the city from terror by air. But opponents disagree, since Daley has wanted to build a park on the airport land for years.

Re-elected for a fifth term as Chicago's mayor in 2003, Richard M. Daley is becoming an Illinois politician as influential and powerful as his father once was.

ILLINOIS AND THE NATION

Illinois voters also send two senators and twenty representatives to work on their behalf in the federal government. Of these, 23 percent are women. "Illinois can take pride in the fact that it sent the first African American and woman to the Senate from 1993 to 1998. Carol Moseley Braun went on to become U.S. ambassador to New Zealand from 1999 to 2001," says Janice Cooper, director of a Washington watchdog group.

Carol Moseley Braun is the first black woman to be elected to the U.S. Senate.

Ideally, government officials at every level work together. Joint programs and cooperation among different agencies help bring extra funding and staff to solve local problems. For example, Illinois had the fourth-highest violent crime rate in the nation in 1994. This sent shock waves through state and federal government. U.S. senators Carol Moseley Braun and Paul Simon launched federal appeals against television violence and called for tougher gun-control laws. Governor Jim Edgar signed the 1995 Violence Prevention Act, a new state public-safety program.

The effort extended to local government. Communities such as Wilmette banned gun ownership. At the time, Jeff Schoenberg was a state representative for several suburbs north of Chicago. He refused to bow to the pressure of the state's ten thousand licensed gun dealers, who wanted local gun-control laws overturned. These joint efforts were only the beginning of the long fight to make Illinois streets safer.

LAWS FOR KIDS

Illinois has a history of protecting kids that began in 1899. Before then, children older than seven who had committed crimes were tried by the same courts as adults. If found guilty, they received the same punishment, including being jailed with adult criminals. Illinois created the first separate court for kids and barred children under twelve from serving jail time.

Judge Julian Mack, who served in Chicago's juvenile court system in the early 1900s, worried about kids found guilty of an offense. Instead of punishing the youngster, he considered, "What had best be done in his interest and in the interest of the state to save him from a downward career?"

Today, Illinois has even more laws to protect kids. Stores cannot sell cigarettes to anyone under eighteen years. Only children sixteen or older can work, unless they are part of a special program. Even then, laws limit the number of hours and the type of work they can do. More recent state laws punish divorced parents who refuse to pay for raising their children. Safe houses and hotlines dealing with child abuse and runaways have been set up across the state to help kids in trouble.

Illinois laws grant kids certain rights. Youths can vote at age eighteen. They can take driver's education at age fifteen and apply for a driver's license at age sixteen. In return, they must be good citizens by following state laws, including wearing their seat belts when riding in vehicles.

Police officers spend time in some of the state's schools, helping students and teaching children how to stay safe.

Illinois kids attend school between the ages of seven and sixteen. They are required to pass a test on the U.S. and Illinois constitutions before graduating eighth grade.

Illinois sponsors several programs to help kids protect themselves. In 1997 several towns in the state began to crack down on teenagers who possess or buy cigarettes. If caught, some had to perform community service work. Another program, D.A.R.E. (Drug Abuse Resistance Education), is the state's most wide-reaching youth program, serving about one million students every year. Police departments train officers who go into elementary, junior high, and high schools to counter media and peer pressure to smoke cigarettes, drink alcohol, and take drugs. Officers also try to help kids resist gangs, violence, and the problems they cause by boosting their self-confidence. A follow-up study of the D.A.R.E. program found that kids who participate have higher grades and fewer fights than those who do not. Through D.A.R.E., Illinois wants kids prepared to make the best choices for their lives. After all, they are the future of Illinois.

Chapter Five

Illinoisans at Work

"Since the 1960s, we went from a sleepy rural town to regional trade center of 15,000 but serving 90,000 people," Marion's chamber of commerce director claims. "We have a diverse economy of government services and industry plus the perfect location along the highway for travel."

Illinois's main strength is its varied economy. Agriculture, manufacturing, mining, and, of course, transportation still account for portions of the state's income. But Illinois workers have adapted to service and technology industries, which are slowly becoming the focus of the nation's economy.

SERVICE INDUSTRIES

Anyone who helps other workers perform their duties holds a service job. Illinois has a record number of jobs in government and university programs, hospitals, law and insurance companies, banks, and media businesses. Service workers account for three-fourths of the jobs in Illinois.

And that includes kids, too. Charles Hays created the School Safety Patrol in 1920 when he was president of Chicago-based AAA Motor Club. Since then, millions of children have served as crossing guards.

A worker inspects an antenna high atop a Chicago skyscraper.

Hands fly as traders buy and sell company stocks on the trading floor in Chicago. The city is an important international business center.

Patrol boys and girls are credited with saving countless lives by helping other kids cross streets on their way to and from school.

With almost half the state's population, the Chicago area has the greatest number of service jobs. More health and medical associations keep their headquarters there than in any region outside of Washington, D.C. Chicago claims the nation's largest printer, RR Donnelley, as well as the second-oldest mail-order house and largest nineteenth-century retailer, Sears, Roebuck and Company, which continues to operate a chain of department stores today. The first mail-order company, Montgomery Ward, was born in Chicago, too. But it closed in 2000.

Even with city businesses closing or moving, Chicago remains the financial capital of the Midwest. Four major Chicago financial institutions, including the Midwest Stock Exchange, monitor our nation's businesses. Buyers and sellers trade more goods at the Chicago Board of Trade than anywhere else in the world.

Illinois tourism is another important part of the state's economy. Lawmakers provide visitor centers throughout the state and maintain Web sites to help travelers locate the best stops, hotels, and entertainment. Visitors spend over $15 billion each year in Illinois, making it one of the ten most visited states.

2003 GROSS STATE PRODUCT: $499 BILLION

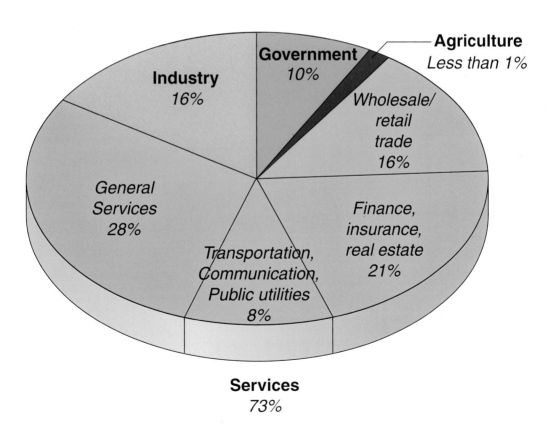

Overseas travelers rank Illinois the seventh most popular state to visit in the United States. Nearly two million foreign visitors made Illinois their travel choice in 2002. The Illinois Trade Office heavily promotes the state in foreign countries in order to boost business and vacation travel.

Chicago draws a large share of the world's travelers. Chicago's O'Hare Airport is the second-busiest in the world after Hartsfield Airport in Atlanta, handling more than 160,000 passengers each day. But the big city is not the only lure to travelers. Smaller towns offer state parks, local attractions, historic sites, and homegrown products as a way to attract visitors to the lesser known areas of the state.

FERTILE FIELDS AND PRODUCTIVE MINES

Few of Illinois's workers farm for a living. Yet Illinois is among the top seven agriculture states nationwide. Farmers send more of their products overseas than from any other state except Iowa. Illinoisans are the country's second-leading producers of soybean and corn behind Iowa. Illinois growers also turn more bushels of corn into ethanol than any other state, making Illinois the leading producer of the gas.

Livestock is another key part of the state's farm industry. Illinois farmers raise a variety of animals, from beef and dairy cattle, hogs, chickens, and turkeys to buffalo, mink, and catfish. Northern Illinois farmers mainly raise hogs, the state's chief meat animal. They also produce Swiss cheese and seeds and bulbs, especially gladioli. Cobden peaches, Murphysboro apples, and Sycamore pumpkins give this part of the state reasons to show off their popular local products with yearly festivals.

Illinois is blessed with the nation's greatest variety of underground resources. Galena once produced 85 percent of the nation's lead. Today, some lead and zinc mines can still be found there. The state also produces the most fluorite in the world. Fluorite, which is used to make steel, glass, and chemicals, is the state's second leading mineral.

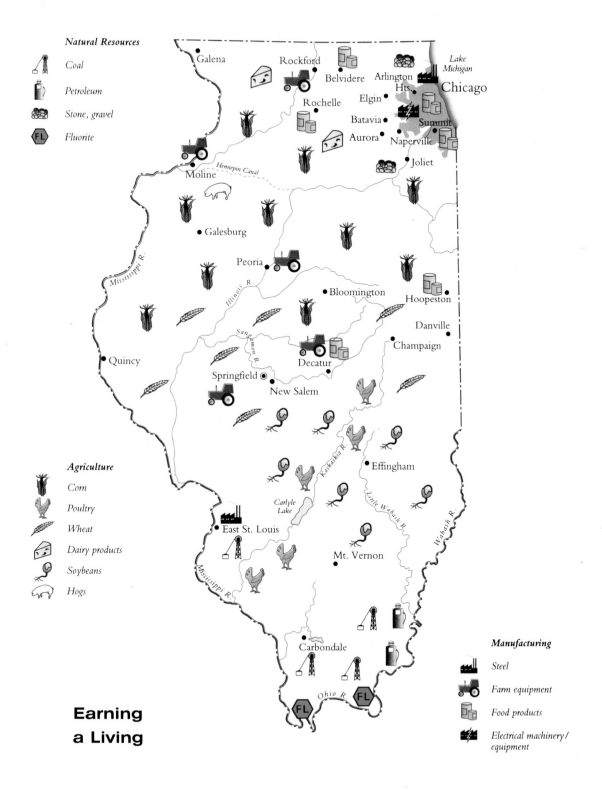

Natural Resources

Coal

Petroleum

Stone, gravel

FL Fluorite

Agriculture

Corn

Poultry

Wheat

Dairy products

Soybeans

Hogs

Manufacturing

Steel

Farm equipment

Food products

Electrical machinery/ equipment

Galena
Rockford
Belvidere
Arlington Hts.
Elgin
Chicago
Lake Michigan
Rochelle
Batavia
Aurora
Summit
Naperville
Joliet
Moline
Hennepin Canal
Galesburg
Peoria
Illinois R.
Bloomington
Hoopeston
Sangamon R.
Danville
Champaign
Decatur
Quincy
Springfield
New Salem
Mississippi R.
Kaskaskia R.
Effingham
Carlyle Lake
Little Wabash R.
Wabash R.
East St. Louis
Mt. Vernon
Mississippi R.
Carbondale
Ohio R.
FL
FL

Earning a Living

This young farmer waits as the cows get milked on a farm near Roodhouse. Dairy farms are important to the state's economy.

Illinois has a surprising amount of oil. Most oil wells are found in the southeast. Still, oil supplies less than 2 percent of the state's energy. Nuclear power furnishes 55 percent of the electric power. The rest comes from coal, the state's main mineral treasure.

Coal lies below two-thirds of the state, providing much of Illinois's mining wealth. Six percent of the nation's coal comes from mines in southern Illinois. The most famous coal mine of all, however, is in the Museum of Science and Industry in Chicago—a model of a real mine that everyone can visit.

PUMPKIN DELIGHTS

Toasted Pumpkin Seeds

Illinois is the number one pumpkin-growing state. While Morton proclaims itself Pumpkin Capital of the World, Sycamore claims the World's Greatest Pumpkin Festival. Native Americans first grew pumpkins and roasted the seeds hundreds of years ago. You can too.

Just scoop the seeds from inside the pumpkin and wash them. Spread the seeds on a greased cookie sheet. Shake salt lightly over them.

Ask an adult to set the oven to about 200° Fahrenheit. Then toast the seeds in the oven until they look dry, which should take about 30 minutes. Let the seeds cool for a while. Then try not to eat them all at once.

Pumpkin Dip

Making pumpkin dip is just one of the many ways the townspeople of Sycamore use their pumpkins.

1. Place 2 cups of mashed pumpkin and 8 ounces of either cream cheese or sour cream into a large bowl.
2. Mix the pumpkin and sour cream until smooth.
3. Add these ingredients to the mixture until smooth and creamy:
    1 cup brown sugar
    1 teaspoon cinnamon
    $1/2$ teaspoon ginger
    $1/2$ teaspoon nutmeg
4. Put the mixture in the refrigerator for at least 4 hours to blend the spices.
5. Serve with crackers, vegetables such as celery and carrots, or gingerbread.

FARM TOOLS, FOODS, AND STEEL MILLS

One in six Illinois jobs is in manufacturing. Illinois factories produce equipment that is exported around the world. The top five industries for export include machinery, computers, chemicals, food products, and transportation equipment. Farm and construction machinery account for the largest share.

John Deere started his tractor company in Grand Detour more than 150 years ago. Now it is an international corporation with headquarters in Moline. Caterpillar in Peoria ranks among the world's major manufacturers of construction equipment, with divisions overseas. Other large equipment and car factories developed in Peoria, Normal, and Belvidere.

Illinois continues to be a leading food-processing state. The state ranks fifth in the nation in total agricultural exports. Meat packing, soybean

Row upon row of chocolates are made in this Chicago factory. Many candy companies are housed in the city.

processing, dairy product manufacturing, and vegetable processing contribute to that honor. Many companies that pioneered chewing gum, hot dogs, and candy bars began in the Chicago area. Today, candy, meat, and dairy products are prepared in factories statewide along with household goods and parts for telephones, computers, and cars.

A CHANGING ECONOMY

Since the 1970s, many of Illinois's large factories have closed, moved, or cut staff. Changes in factory methods plus cheaper labor and raw materials available elsewhere meant some older factories could not compete. The factory closings that resulted came as a terrible blow to most communities.

During the 1980s, many steel mills outside Chicago started shutting down. The air around the mills cleared without smokestacks spitting out smelly gases. But the loss of mills cost many jobs. Without wages to buy goods, stores closed and people moved away. Nearby neighborhoods decayed.

BROOM CORN BROOMS

Did you know that Illinois was once the broom corn capital of the world? Fields of broom corn, which looks like regular corn stalks, covered central Illinois. A major broom-producing industry grew up around the town of Arcola.

"The problem was broom corn needed about three hundred people to harvest," remembers Alvin Wingler, president of Warren Broom Company. "Farmers could make more money growing corn."

Many of the nation's brooms are still handmade in Arcola. Mexican yucca plant fibers have replaced most midwestern broom corn. But Arcola still celebrates its role in making brooms with an annual Broom Corn Festival.

ILLINOIS WORKFORCE

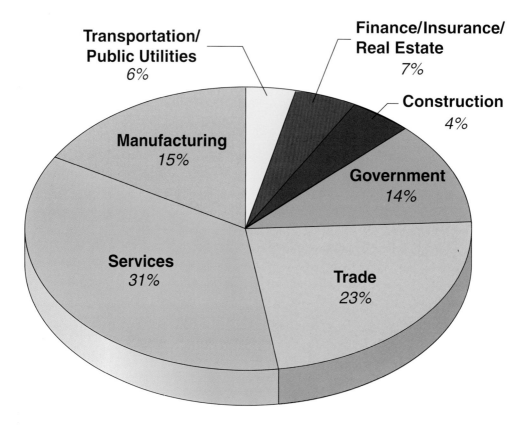

Transportation/Public Utilities 6%

Finance/Insurance/Real Estate 7%

Construction 4%

Manufacturing 15%

Government 14%

Services 31%

Trade 23%

"Ma and pa businesses struggled," said one Hegewisch resident. "People traveled downtown for jobs or went into service industries as police and firefighters."

Today, local leaders are still working to tear down abandoned steel mills. They hope to develop the land into other businesses and create new jobs for the people of south Chicago.

Service workers faced similar challenges after the federal government closed several military bases, including Rantoul's seventy-six-year-old air force base. Rantoul's population of 17,000 dropped by 5,000 people. Townspeople who worked at the base lost their jobs. In the end Rantoul was left with thousands of acres of unused land.

"We had more problems than if a factory closed," remembered former mayor Katy Podagrosi. "The base had a hospital, water system, electricity, airport, and 1,400 houses. We acquired a full city within a city."

Over the next five years, kids said good-bye to longtime friends. At home, many children worried about parents who had lost their jobs.

City and federal planners acted quickly to design a new community. By 1995 Rantoul attracted more than 2,500 jobs at seven major companies housed on the base. Social services, education and recreation, and business offices filled the buildings. Hangar Four became an aerospace museum, the first in Illinois, complete with combat jets and a missile silo.

Where in the world are we? This suburban Chicago factory specializes in making globes.

"Rantoul feels good about itself," Podagrosi said. "The country feels good about us, too."

Illinois lawmakers work to find new business for all areas of the state. They participate in yearly fairs in Mexico City to promote Illinois industries in Latin America. Government and business leaders regularly visit overseas companies. They want foreign companies to open factories in the state and to buy Illinois products. Illinois sends it products to 228 countries and ranks first in the Midwest in bringing foreign businesses to the United States. Even when the national economy is bad, people from Illinois find a way to thrive.

PROTECTING THE ENVIRONMENT

Illinois has a terrible record when it comes to protecting the environment. Factories, businesses, and heavily populated cities take a great toll on natural resources. In addition, Illinois allots less money than most states for protecting its resources.

In 1995 the state introduced a program to raise money for state parks. Car and truck owners can choose special license plates decorated with the colorful state bird, the cardinal, and the state prairie grass, big bluestem. These plates cost more, but the extra money goes to improve parks and hire park workers.

Problems with the Illinois environment go beyond not having enough money, however. In 1997 state lawmakers passed a bill that allows companies to dump their waste in ordinary city waste sites. This saves companies a lot of money but adds to the possible air, water, and land pollution that the state will eventually have to address.

Another waste problem is the garbage created by neighborhoods and communities. Every person in Illinois produces more than a ton of garbage per year. Waste seeps into the ground and water supply, changing the environment and possibly harming plants and animals.

Old traditions and new technologies mix as farmers use cell phones to aid them during harvesttime.

Illinois is running out of places to put its waste. Towns battle over where to bury garbage. Once the state was mostly flatland. Now more than 117 landfills have created grassed-covered mounds of garbage at sites across the state.

In 1990 state lawmakers adopted a series of laws to limit harmful waste. Grass clippings and leaves can no longer be burned. Instead, they are left on the lawn, saved for compost, or hauled away to create giant compost piles.

This girl is doing her part to ensure Illinois has a bright and healthy future. This white pine seedling will one day grow into a tree covered in needles.

Many local districts run strict programs when it comes to reusing and recycling waste. Homeowners and businesses separate plastic, paper, glass, and metal containers for garbage pickups. Then the materials are taken to recycling centers.

Other laws address problems of factory waste spoiling air and water. Counties with recreation areas restrict hunting and fishing. Major efforts go into listing, identifying, and saving endangered plants and animals.

In Chicago, rows of trees planted along busy highways help absorb the fumes given off by cars. City planners cleaned the muddy Chicago River. The giant Deep Tunnel project improved sewage treatment, making the river a pleasant "second lakefront." Greenery grew so thick that deer and wolves returned to the river's north branch.

Illinois lawmakers believe that kids hold the key to protecting the environment. The state trains teachers to help kids enjoy and save nature. The Department of Conservation holds Arbor Day contests and publishes fun nature-related materials. Illinois wants kids involved in the future of their state.

Chapter Six
Illinois Highlights

"I love it here," beams one newcomer from the East Coast. "The state combines the hectic pace of big eastern cities like Philadelphia with southern gentility. The people look at you and make eye contact: they're really friendly."

Touring Illinois is a treat. With good trains, highways, and airports, traveling is easier here than in many other places. And people around the state welcome visitors. They are eager and proud to share the things they love best about Illinois.

CHICAGO

"When I lived in Atlanta, I felt I was living in the state of Georgia," notes Ohio-born author Arlene Erlbach. "In Illinois, I have the feeling of living in Chicago."

For many people, Illinois is Chicago. It is the nation's third-largest city and is home to a majority of the state's manufacturing and service industries as well as much of the population. Its colorful ethnic neighborhoods, grand monuments and buildings, festivals, parks, beaches, and

A statue of a young Abraham Lincoln stands watch. The state is often called the Land of Lincoln.

museums rival any in the world. With the bustle of big business and its busy downtown and neighborhood streets, people never get bored.

"The best part of living in Illinois is the city of Chicago as the center of culture," observes tour guide Steve Berger.

Any type of entertainment can be found there. The Chicago Symphony Orchestra and Chicago Symphony Chorus perform to sold-out audiences in the winter. Both fill Orchestra Hall at downtown's Symphony Center with magical sounds. By summer, the world-class orchestra moves outdoors to Ravinia in suburban Highland Park.

But the musical styles that most represent Chicago are jazz and blues. Chicago holds its own separate jazz and blues festivals. "This is a place for music and a great place for jazz. That's why I've been here all these years," says jazz pianist Ramsey Lewis.

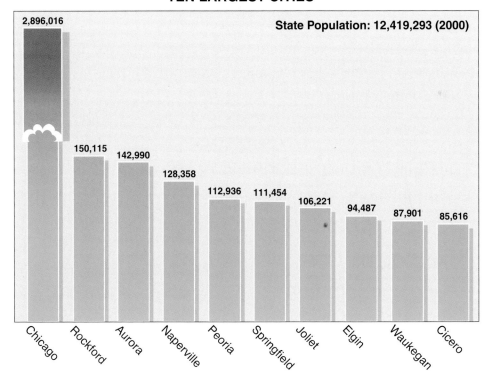

TEN LARGEST CITIES

State Population: 12,419,293 (2000)

Chicago	2,896,016
Rockford	150,115
Aurora	142,990
Naperville	128,358
Peoria	112,936
Springfield	111,454
Joliet	106,221
Elgin	94,487
Waukegan	87,901
Cicero	85,616

Dance companies, such as the lively Hubbard Street, the Lyric Opera, and many theaters and clubs offer enjoyment for every taste. The best in home-grown talent comes from Second City, a group that set many standards for comedy. Second City developed Chicago's special form of humor called improvisation. Improv, for short, is performed spur of the moment. After each show, the actors ask the audience to suggest what they should act out. The best scenes are often added to the regular show.

Second City has become so popular that it blossomed in Chicago suburbs and other big cities. The comedy group helped start the careers of many film and television actors, especially comics featured on *Saturday Night Live*. Bill Murray of Wilmette, Dan Aykroyd, and Harold Ramis are all Second City graduates.

According to the Chicago *Tribune*, "There are few things we find funny that can't be traced back to some Second City source."

Chicago is also a great place for sports lovers. They can watch professional teams and Special Olympics events in large stadiums and play polo, soccer, and volleyball in the lakefront park. One hundred years ago, city planners developed Chicago's 29 miles of shoreline into a tree-lined skyline of parks, museums, and recreation areas. On hot summer days, people flock from every neighborhood to cool off at lakefront beaches. They picnic, rollerblade, bicycle, fish, golf, and jog. Many families crowd Lincoln Park Zoo, one of the few free large urban zoos left in the country.

Downtown's Grant Park and new Millennium Park make up the city's "front lawn." Free music concerts can be heard many summer nights. After the music, colorful dancing lights spout from nearby Buckingham Fountain. Almost every summer weekend, the park comes alive with festivals that showcase local gifts. In addition to jazz and blues, visitors can hear gospel, bagpipers, and Latin beats.

"Over one million people celebrate our beautiful lakefront at Venetian Night. For almost forty years, viewers delighted to the parade of decorated boats and following fireworks," notes a city worker.

GANGSTER HIDEOUTS

Chicago has its share of unusual buildings. The office tower at 35 West Wacker Drive was once a jewelers' building with an elevator big enough to hold a car. That way, the jewelers could drive their cars upstairs without worrying about getting robbed.

Feared gangster Al Capone (left) used the upper four floors for a hangout during the 1920s. It was illegal at the time to buy and sell alcohol throughout the United States. Capone's empire of criminals made and sold liquor. He opened a lively speakeasy, a private drinking club, on the top floor. Anyone who objected was kidnapped, beaten, or killed. Capone finally went to jail for not paying enough taxes. Even then, his mother claimed he was a "good boy."

For years, the murderous Capone gang was all people remembered about Illinois.

The lakefront is home to many outstanding museums. One of these is the Field Museum of Natural History. Its exhibits include mummies and dinosaurs shown at the 1893 world's fair. Now, the museum invites families for sleepovers. Late at night, when lights are low, creepy lifelike creatures encased in glass watch kids eat snacks and curl up in their sleeping bags.

The Field Museum of Natural History houses Sue, the giant Tyrannosaurus rex *fossil. It was discovered in 1990 and, at 5 feet long and with 12-inch teeth, is the largest* T rex *specimen found to date.*

The Art Institute of Chicago was built during the world's fair. Since then, the museum has assembled a world-famous collection of paintings, sculpture, and crafts. Even kids who dislike museums love the weekend family art projects, armor collection, and Thorne miniature rooms.

Chicago is known for its architecture and amazing buildings. The Chicago school of architecture produced such famous architects as Louis Sullivan and Daniel Burnham. They created landmarks from the ashes of the Chicago fire of 1871. Burnham ordered, "Make no little plans: they have no magic to stir men's blood."

Chicago's downtown business district is an outdoor architecture museum. In creating it, local architects revolutionized building design with their use of steel beams and glass. William Le Baron Jenney built the first skyscraper with a metal frame. In 1885 his ten-story Home Insurance Building became a model for future skyscrapers. Today, the Rookery by Daniel Burnham and John Root stands as the world's oldest metal-framed skyscraper.

This part of town is called the Loop, named for the elevated train tracks that ring or "loop" the district. The Loop displays fresh ideas in building that keep the ideals of the Chicago school of architecture alive. Modern architects top their buildings with beehive shapes, geometric designs, or domes that look like plastic balls. Towering above them all in the downtown skyline is the 110-story Sears Tower. At 1,453 feet, the building ranks among the tallest in the world. From 1974 to 1996, the tower held that title.

Wide plazas between grand office buildings feature sculpture from other world-famous artists. Claes Oldenburg, who taught at the Art Institute, created the sporty, gray *Bat Column*, a giant hollow metal base-ball bat, in front of a federal building. Spanish artist Pablo Picasso gave Chicago a huge metal sculpture for its Civic Center plaza. After decades, passersby still ask, "What is that?"

At 1,453 feet, the Sears Tower is the king of the Chicago skyline.

Lighthearted sculptures are sprinkled throughout downtown and lakefront parks. The northwestern suburb of Skokie liked Chicago's idea of displaying art everyone can enjoy. City leaders created sculpture gardens in the park along the Chicago River and in the Old Orchard shopping mall.

Chicago recycles its relics. Warehouses become indoor golf courses, restaurants, and museums. The lakefront's three-quarter-mile-long Navy Pier, built originally for shipping and then a university, is now a lively lakefront playground. It contains the Chicago Children's Museum, an IMAX movie theater, a carousel, and outdoor stage. A 150-foot-high Ferris wheel with 16,000 lights overlooks the harbor and the city's skyline.

The "Magnificent Mile," a stretch of elegant shops, runs along North Michigan Avenue. Off that main boulevard is a city visitor center in the historic waterworks, one of the few remaining buildings to survive the great Chicago fire. Each winter holiday season, the street shimmers with thousands of white lights. They beckon to adventurers who seek out the city's nightlife on nearby Rush Street.

Author Andrew Greeley wrote how "you have to poke around the neighborhoods to know Chicago." Chicago is a city of neighborhoods. Unlike the suburbs where cars and shopping malls rule, Chicagoans travel by foot, bus, and public train. Neighborhoods reveal their own personality in the houses, stores, restaurants, libraries, and languages spoken in the streets. Jane Addams's Hull House is still open as a museum near the University of Illinois, a monument to neighborhood cooperation.

On the South Side is the 1,055-acre Jackson Park, site of the 1893 world's fair. The giant stone Museum of Science and Industry reminds visitors of how grand the event was. Today, the museum exhibits a World War II submarine, hatching chickens, and a real 727 jet plane. With about 2 million visitors per year, this is one of the city's most popular museums.

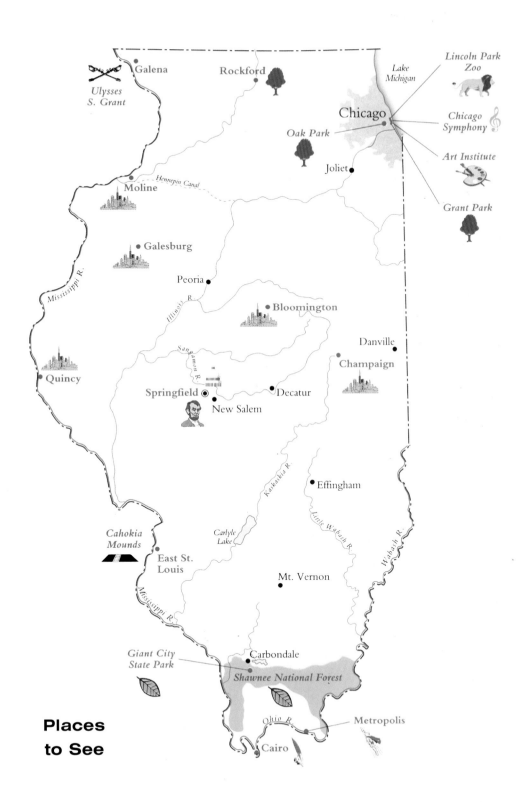

Galena

*Ulysses
S. Grant*

Rockford

*Lake
Michigan*

Lincoln Park
Zoo

Chicago

*Chicago
Symphony*

Oak Park

Joliet

Art Institute

Moline

Hennepin Canal

Grant Park

Galesburg

Peoria

Illinois R.

Bloomington

Danville

Mississippi R.

Sangamon R.

Champaign

Quincy

Springfield

New Salem

Decatur

Kaskaskia R.

Effingham

Little Wabash R.

Wabash R.

*Carlyle
Lake*

*Cahokia
Mounds*

East St.
Louis

Mt. Vernon

Mississippi R.

*Giant City
State Park*

Carbondale

Shawnee National Forest

Ohio R.

Metropolis

Cairo

**Places
to See**

Murals combine art, history, and ethnic pride in this Chicago neighborhood. The city's Latino heritage is rich, with deep roots.

FIESTA DEL SOL

According to Helen Valdez, founder of the Mexican Fine Arts Center Museum in the Pilsen neighborhood, Chicago has "the fastest-growing population of Latinos" in the United States. For five days each summer, the community holds Fiesta del Sol to honor their culture. Fiesta del Sol features more than one hundred booths with foods, rides, and crafts—a carnival atmosphere. It is the biggest Mexican festival in the United States.

Nearby Hyde Park boasts higher learning at the stately University of Chicago campus. Perhaps that's why the community hosts a large book fair each year and has three one-of-a-kind museums. The DuSable Museum of African American History traces the black presence in America.

Closer to downtown is the Spanish-speaking neighborhood of Pilsen, located near Harrison Park. An abstract orange steel Puerto Rican flag waves over Division Street. A converted boat repair shop houses the country's largest museum dedicated to Mexican culture, the Mexican Fine Arts Center Museum. Not so far away is the Peace Museum, the only art and history museum dedicated solely to peace. Its exhibits of art, music—including Beatle John Lennon's guitar—and writing explore how to achieve world peace. The museum offers a school program that helps kids learn to resolve conflicts peacefully.

The city and suburbs celebrate their ethnic roots with music, food, crafts, parades, and carnivals. Greek town, Little Italy, the Scandinavian area of Andersonville, and Chinatown each contain blocks of active restaurants that feature their nationality's food. Evanston holds an Ethnic Fair for all groups. Russian stacking dolls mingle with Nicaraguan hammocks, while African dancers bounce to pounding drums.

During the late 1800s, a New Yorker called Chicago the "Windy City." People thought the name suggested the gusty winds that blow off Lake Michigan. The man really referred to the "windy" Chicagoans who brag so much about their city. After a visit to Chicago, it is no wonder the natives are so proud of their hometown.

NORTHERN ILLINOIS

Suburbs flow out of Chicago for miles. Chicago-style comedy, music, and theater productions have blossomed far from their downtown Chicago roots. In addition, each community celebrates its own hometown heroes and history. Oak Park is the birthplace of author Ernest Hemingway, and internationally known architect Frank Lloyd Wright created his early building designs there.

Wright believed buildings should fit their surroundings. Therefore, he designed structures that were low and wide like Illinois's prairie, rather than tall like skyscrapers. He used bricks and wood that blended into landscapes. His work became known as the "Prairie Style," and Oak Park has more examples of his talents than anywhere else in the United States.

Ninety minutes northwest of Chicago is Rockford, Illinois's second-largest city. The town began in 1834 when a dam was built over the Rock River for a sawmill. The "rock ford" offered travelers a way to cross the river between Chicago and Galena. The name stuck.

Rockford is mainly a manufacturing city. There are a few museums and an annual riverfront festival. The main attraction, however, is trees. Rockford averages one hundred trees for every city block. Citizens call their hometown the City of Trees.

Churches and homes hug the steep hillsides of Galena, an historic Illinois mining town.

**Illinois
by County**

Train lovers flock to nearby Union and its Illinois Railway Museum. They can see 250 cars and locomotives, including the last Chicago streetcar taken out of service in 1958. But most visitors prefer to boat, fish, and camp in the region's more than 160 parks.

Galena re-creates the history of northwestern Illinois. It is known as "the town that time forgot." The clock stopped during the 1850s when Galena was a mining and riverboat boomtown of 15,000 people and Chicago only a clump of cabins.

Today, the area's four thousand residents embrace life as it was. Much of the main street has been restored. Most of the town's old mansions and buildings are national historic sites. The house that the city awarded to Civil War hero General Ulysses S. Grant is a major tourist stop.

CENTRAL ILLINOIS

"Kids from Jacksonville take Lincoln stuff for granted," remembers Becky Todd. "Their field trips are to Springfield, Lincoln's tomb, and New Salem. They often don't understand why visitors from other states are interested in Lincoln places."

Central Illinois is the Land of Lincoln. The region has more historic sites than the other parts of the state combined. This is not only because Springfield is the state capital. People also visit to see where Abraham Lincoln lived, worked, and is buried.

New Salem along the Sangamon River was where Lincoln lived from 1831 to 1837. In 1933 a federal program re-created the town on its original foundations. Today, the log village serves as a reminder of life in Lincoln's time, as guides tell secrets about Lincoln and his neighbors. Girls wear puffy-sleeved dresses with awkward billowy skirts, and boys put on warm buckskin pants and rabbit caps, even in summer. They explain what it was like to spend your whole life—eating, sleeping, cooking, and sewing—in one room, sometimes shared with animals.

This home in downtown Springfield, once owned by Abraham Lincoln and his wife, is open to the public and a popular stop for visitors.

Fifteen miles away is Springfield. The only home Lincoln ever owned is on Jackson and 8th streets. His law offices still stand nearby. They are furnished with a combination of what the family owned and what they might have sold before leaving for Washington, D.C. The home's parlor is set up for the social events that the Lincoln's often hosted. They were known to arrange popular strawberry parties, times when friends gathered to eat strawberries and cream.

Springfield has several grand state buildings. Lincoln argued more than two hundred cases before the Illinois supreme court in the Old State Capitol. But the state capitol that began construction in 1868 is the current hub of government.

Illinois's capitol extends three city blocks and is 74 feet taller than the national Capitol. Each picture, marking, and statue captures an important feature in Illinois history, such as the statue of the first female state legislator, Lottie Holman O'Neill, first elected in 1922. Pictures of Abraham Lincoln and Stephen Douglas on different sides of the house chamber show lawmakers where to sit. Republicans sit on Lincoln's side, and Democrats sit on Douglas's side.

Outside of Springfield is Lincoln's tomb in Oak Ridge Cemetery. He is buried with his wife, Mary, and three of their sons. Lincoln's famous speeches are inscribed on bronze plaques. One tells of the new president leaving his beloved home. He said of his Springfield neighbors, "to the kindest of these people I owe everything."

A bust of Abraham Lincoln keeps watch over his tomb in Springfield's Oak Ridge Cemetery.

A canoe gliding along the Cache River provides the perfect way of exploring the Shawnee National Forest.

SOUTHERN ILLINOIS

At first, the girls at Mount Vernon's Wheels Through Time Museum just smiled. "You want to know what we do for fun? Well," laughed one of them, "we have frog races for excitement."

Then they thought some more, and their pride swelled about southern Illinois. The greatest treasure they agreed was in the Shawnee National Forest. "You've got to see the Garden of the Gods," one exclaimed. The ancient rock formation is a favorite spot where teenagers often gather.

Scientists estimate that 15 million baskets of earth were used over a three-hundred-year period to build Monks Mound at Cahokia Mounds in west-central Illinois. The mound gets its name from the monastery and farm French monks built there in the early eighteenth century.

"And you must walk through Giant City," the other girl bubbled. These rock designs were part of the larger Giant City State Park. The park was named for the huge rock walls that look like shaded streets. Native Americans lived in the bluffs almost ten thousand years ago. Ceilings blackened from their fires can still be seen today.

The most striking reminder of Indian life is Cahokia Mounds Historic Site near East Saint Louis. A movie, detailed dioramas, and live demonstrations at the visitor center bring Native American history to life. Then the real journey into history begins—exploring the mounds on foot and imagining what Illinois was like more than nine hundred years ago.

Illinois has more wonderful treasures than one book could possibly cover. Historic landmarks can be found across the state. Grand courthouses have beautified town squares for more than one hundred years. Their splendor recalls each town's special past. People of the original "Prairie State" and historic "Land of Lincoln" would most likely agree that, as Chicago author L. Frank Baum wrote in *The Wonderful Wizard of Oz*, "There is no place like home."

ILLINOIS

THE FLAG: The state flag, which shows the state seal on a white background, was first adopted in 1915. The state name was added in 1969.

THE SEAL: In the center of the state seal is an American eagle holding a shield containing stars and stripes for the thirteen original colonies. The eagle holds a banner bearing the state's motto in its beak. Olive branches under the shield symbolize peace. A nearby boulder has two dates: 1818, the year Illinois entered the Union, and 1868, the year the seal was adopted.

State Survey

Statehood: December 3, 1818

Origin of Name: Illinois is French for Illiniwek, the name of the group of Native Americans who lived in the region before the coming of white settlers.

Nickname: Prairie State, Land of Lincoln

Capital: Springfield

Motto: State Sovereignty, National Union

Bird: Cardinal

Animal: White-tailed deer

Fish: Bluegill

Insect: Monarch butterfly

Flower: Purple violet

Tree: White oak

Mineral: Fluorite

Fossil: Tully monster

Dance: Square dance

Prairie Grass: Big bluestem

White-tailed deer

ILLINOIS

State residents have considered "Illinois" their state song from the time it was written by Charles H. Chamberlain, sometime between 1890 and 1893. Chamberlain had set his words to a melody written by Archibald Johnson in 1870 in the hope that his lyrics coupled with Johnson's familiar tune would help bring the 1893 World's Columbian Exposition to Chicago. In 1925 Florence Fifer Bohner, the state's first female senator, introduced a motion to proclaim "Illinois" the official state song. It was adopted on June 25, 1925.

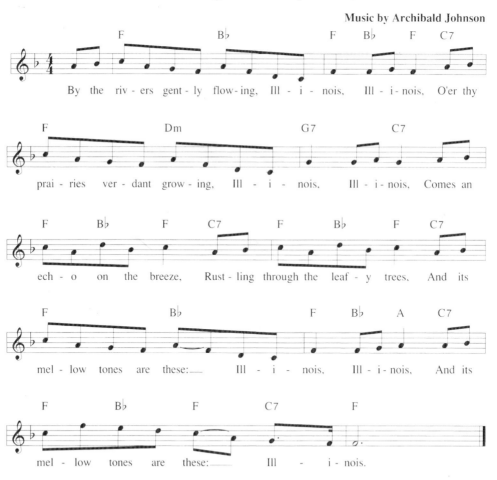

Music by Archibald Johnson

GEOGRAPHY

Highest Point: 1,235 feet above sea level, at Charles Mound

Lowest Point: 279 feet above sea level, along the Mississippi River in southern Illinois

Area: 55,645 square miles

Greatest Distance, North to South: 385 miles

Greatest Distance, East to West: 220 miles

Bordering States: Wisconsin to the north, Iowa to the west, Missouri to the southwest, Kentucky to the southeast, and Indiana to the east

Hottest Recorded Temperature: 117° F, at East Saint Louis on July 14, 1954

Coldest Recorded Temperature: -36° F, at Congerville on January 5, 1999

Average Annual Precipitation: 38 inches

Major Rivers: Mississippi, Illinois, Wabash, Chicago, Des Plaines, Rock, Vermilion, Fox, Sangamon, Spoon, Kankakee, Embarras, Big Muddy, Kaskaskia, Pecatonica, Calumet, Kishwaukee

Major Lakes: Michigan, Carlyle, Crab Orchard, Rend, Chain O'Lakes, Goose, Peoria, Senachwine, Springfield, Decatur, Bloomington, Lake of Egypt, Shelbyville

Trees: oak, white oak, hickory, elm, ash, cottonwood, walnut, maple, birch, beech, sycamore, bald cypress, tupelo

Wild Plants: violet, wild barley, gumweed, wild geranium, bluebell, chess, bloodroot, Dutchman's-breeches, toothwort, snow trillium, goldenrod

Animals: white-tailed deer, fox squirrel, thirteen-lined ground squirrel, cottontail rabbit, raccoon, red fox, gray fox, beaver, Virginia opossum, striped skunk, mink, muskrat, badger, bobcat, common snapping turtle, coyote, eastern chipmunk, least weasel, long-tailed weasel, pocket gopher, red bat, river otter, short-tailed shrew, white-footed mouse

Red foxes

Barn owl

Birds: cardinal, sparrow, bluejay, barn owl, American crow, chickadee, red-winged blackbird, hummingbird, bobwhite quail, ring-neck pheasant, Canada goose, great blue heron, wood duck, mallard, swallow, hawk, turkey, belted kingfisher, woodpecker

Fish: bluegill, carp, catfish, largemouth and smallmouth bass, redear sunfish, crappie, perch, white bass, walleye, sauger, bullhead, buffalo fish, northern pike, salmon, lake trout, muskellunge

Threatened and Endangered Animals: Illinois cave amphipod, gray bat, Indiana bat, Karner blue butterfly, Hine's emerald dragonfly, bald eagle, fanshell, Higgins' eye (mussel), pink mucket (mussel), orange-foot pimpleback (mussel), piping plover, fat pocketbook (mussel), Iowa Pleistocene snail, pallid sturgeon, least tern, gray wolf

Endangered and Threatened Plants: Mead's milkweed, decurrent false aster, Pitcher's thistle, lakeside daisy, prairie bush clover, small whorled pogonia, eastern prairie fringed orchid, leafy prairie-clover

TIMELINE

about 1500 Illiniweks live in the region that will become Illinois

1673 Jolliet and Marquette explore Illinois

1680 La Salle builds Fort Crèvecoeur near the present site of Peoria

1699 Settlement of Cahokia founded

1703 Settlement of Kaskaskia founded

1763 British troops enter Illinois and take control of the region from the French

1778 George Rogers Clark captures Kaskaskia from the British

1779 Du Sable constructs a trading post at the present-day site of Chicago

1779 Settlers from Maryland and Virginia establish the first English-speaking settlement in Illinois, near present-day Waterloo

1787 Illinois becomes part of the Northwest Territory according to the Northwest Ordinance, in which Congress rules that the region will eventually be divided into a number of states

1809 Territory of Illinois created

1818 Illinois becomes a state

1832 Black Hawk War ends Native American resistance in Illinois

1834 Abraham Lincoln elected to the Illinois house of representatives

1837 Illinois capital moves from Vandalia to Springfield

1858 Abraham Lincoln and Stephen A. Douglas hold a series of debates as they campaign for U.S. senator

1860 Abraham Lincoln elected president of the United States

1861 Civil War begins

1863 Emancipation Proclamation

1865 Lincoln assassinated in Washington, D.C., and buried in Springfield

1871 Great Chicago Fire

1886 Haymarket Riot in Chicago

1889 Jane Addams's Hull House opens in Chicago

1893 The World's Columbian Exposition opens in Chicago

1919 Race riots erupt in Chicago

1929 Great Depression begins

1933 A Century of Progress Exposition opens in Chicago

1968 Gwendolyn Brooks becomes poet laureate of Illinois

1971 Abraham Lincoln's Springfield home recognized as a national historic site

1973 The world's tallest building, the Sears Tower, completed in Chicago

1983 Harold Washington, Chicago's first black mayor, elected

1993 Millions of acres of Illinois farmland damaged by Mississippi flooding

2003 Governor George Ryan changes the sentences of all prisoners facing the death penalty in the state

ECONOMY

Potato harvest

Agricultural Products: Corn, soybeans, wheat, oats, hay, apples, peaches, pumpkins, potatoes, hogs, cattle, dairy products, chickens, turkeys, eggs, sheep and lambs

Manufactured Products: Construction machinery, printed products, farm machinery, electrical instruments, appliances, iron and steel, other metals, processed foods, meat products, railroad equipment, automobile parts, chemicals, drugs

Natural Resources: Bituminous coal, crude oil, natural gas, fluorspar, tripoli, zinc, copper, lead, lime, silver, barite, clay, sand and gravel, crushed stone, peat, timber

Business and Trade: Banking, advertising and public relations, insurance, retail sales, transportation, research

CALENDAR OF CELEBRATIONS

Bald Eagle Days This two-day festival comes in January in Rock Island, as bald eagles migrate southward along the Mississippi. Visitors can see live eagles close up in the exhibit hall. Or, eagles can be viewed as they fly and glide along the Mississippi River.

Lincoln Birthday Weekend Every February, Springfield hosts a weekend full of events, including parades and lectures by scholars on Lincoln's life and achievements.

Dutch Days The Dutch heritage of Fulton is celebrated every May with wooden shoe dancing and a parade featuring traditional Dutch costumes.

Superman Celebration Metropolis, the "official home of Superman," hosts a Superman festival every June that includes a live, outdoor Superman show.

Old Canal Days The city of Lockport celebrates its history along the Illinois and Michigan Canal every June with carriage rides and canal walks.

Taste of Chicago Held every June, this celebration showcases all the fantastic foods Chicago has to offer.

Chicago Blues Festival The special strains of the blues fill Chicago's streets in June when the city celebrates its musical roots.

Illinois State Fair August brings the state fair to Springfield along with food, music, rides, racing pigs, a cow carved from butter, and lots of other fun attractions.

Sweet Corn Festival Held every summer in Mendota, a farming community about 80 miles west of Chicago, this August festival serves up about 160,000 ears of corn to visitors.

Chicago Jazz Festival Jazz sounds are celebrated every August in Chicago, where so many jazz musicians got their start.

Rediscover Cahokia Mounds Day

Rediscover Cahokia Mounds Days
Usually held in September, this festival at the Cahokia Mounds celebrates the heritage of the region's Native Americans with dancing and craft demonstrations.

Jordbruksdagarna This September farm festival in the Swedish community of Bishop Hill demonstrates how early settlers harvested crops, the kinds of games they played, and crafts from the 1850s.

Railsplitting Festival The town of Lincoln hosts this tribute to Abraham Lincoln in September. The festival includes a railsplitting contest in honor of Lincoln's legendary skill at splitting logs into fence rails.

Fort Crèvecoeur Rendezvous Every September, fur trappers in buckskins paddle their canoes and fire their flintlock rifles in this festival held at the state historic site.

STATE STARS

Jane Addams (1860–1935) was born in Cedarville and attended Rockford College. Addams opened Hull House, a neighborhood settlement house that offered care and education to the inner-city poor, in Chicago in 1889 after seeing a similar settlement house in London, England. Addams also worked for world peace and in 1931 earned a Nobel Peace Prize for her efforts.

Philip Danforth Armour (1832–1901) helped make Chicago a leader in the meat-packing industry. He founded Armour & Company in 1867 and bragged about using "every part of the pig but the squeal" in his meat products.

Black Hawk (1767–1838) was a leader of the Sauk people. After he was forced to leave the state, Black Hawk returned with a group of his people in 1832, which led to the outbreak of the Black Hawk War. Defeated by U.S. militia, Black Hawk spent the rest of his life in Iowa.

Bonnie Blair (1964–) of Champaign began ice skating when she was two years old. Years of practice helped her become the first woman to earn back-to-back gold medals in Olympic speed skating. Blair won gold medals in the 1988, 1992, and 1994 Winter Olympic Games.

Gwendolyn Brooks (1917–2000) was the first African-American woman poet to win a Pulitzer Prize. Brooks grew up in Chicago, and much of her poetry concerns the life of black Americans. In 1968 Brooks became poet laureate of Illinois.

Gwendolyn Brooks

Edgar Rice Burroughs (1875–1950), the creator of Tarzan, was born in Chicago. Burroughs wrote his first book about the "king of the jungle" in 1912 and wrote twenty-six Tarzan books in all. Burroughs's character has since been featured in many movies and television programs.

Richard J. Daley (1902–1976) was born in Chicago and served as that city's mayor for twenty-one years, from 1955 until his death. Daley was one of the most powerful politicians in America. He controlled Chicago government completely during his years in office.

Miles Davis (1926–1991) is known as one of the world's greatest jazz trumpet players. Born in Alton, Davis had a great influence on jazz styles in the 1950s and 1960s.

John Deere (1804–1886), a blacksmith born in Vermont, invented the first successful steel plow in his workshop in Grand Detour. Deere created his plow from an old saw blade after hearing local farmers complain that Illinois's thick soil stuck to their iron and wood plows. Deere's invention improved farming throughout the Midwest.

Walt Disney

Walt Disney (1901–1966), the creator of Mickey Mouse and Disneyland, was born in Chicago. Although Disney moved from Illinois as a young boy, he returned to study art in Chicago. Among his many full-length animated films are *Snow White and the Seven Dwarfs, Cinderella,* and *Fantasia.*

Stephen A. Douglas (1813–1861), called "the Little Giant," is best known for his senate campaign against Abraham Lincoln in 1858. Douglas moved from Vermont to Illinois in 1833, served in the U.S. House of Representatives from 1843 to 1847, and then in the Senate from 1847 to 1861.

Jean Baptiste Point du Sable (1745–1818) was born in Haiti and was part African and part French. In 1779 du Sable became Chicago's first settler when he built a trading post at the mouth of the Chicago River. Although his trading post was very successful, du Sable mysteriously moved away in 1800.

George Ferris (1859–1896) was born in Galesburg. Ferris built a "pleasure wheel" that stood 264 feet high for the World's Columbian Exposition in Chicago in 1893. Such pleasure wheels soon became known as Ferris wheels.

Marshall Field (1834–1906) opened the Marshall Field & Company store in Chicago. Based on fair pricing and the slogan, "Give the Lady What She Wants," the store became the largest retail establishment in the world. Field gave much back to the community, including $9 million to open the Field Museum of Natural History.

Harrison Ford (1942–), one of Hollywood's most popular actors, was born in Chicago. Ford starred in *Star Wars* and its two sequels. He also played Indiana Jones in *Raiders of the Lost Ark, Indiana Jones and the Temple of Doom,* and *Indiana Jones and the Last Crusade.*

Ernest Hemingway (1899–1961), one of the twentieth century's greatest American authors, was born in Oak Park. Hemingway wrote novels and short stories and received the 1954 Nobel Prize in literature. Some of his best-known works include *A Farewell to Arms, For Whom the Bell Tolls,* and *The Old Man and the Sea.*

Mahalia Jackson (1911–1972) moved to Chicago when she was fifteen years old. A year later, she began singing gospel music and became one of the most popular gospel performers in history. Her million-selling songs include "Move on up a Little Higher," and "He's Got the Whole World in His Hands." Jackson also worked for equal rights for African Americans.

Mae Jemison (1956–) of Chicago became the first black woman astronaut to go into space in 1992. Jemison is a doctor who has volunteered in a Cambodian refugee camp and worked with the Peace Corps in West Africa. Today she helps students discover the wonders of science and space.

Quincy Jones (1933–) of Chicago is one of modern music's most talented artists. As a composer, conductor, and trumpeter, he has won more awards than any other musician of his time. Jones helped write the song "We Are the World" and produced Michael Jackson's album *Thriller.*

Michael Jordan (1963–) is considered by many to be the world's greatest athlete. Raised in North Carolina, Jordan was drafted by the Chicago Bulls in 1984. He helped the Bulls win six basketball championships. His exciting style of play earned him the nickname "Air" Jordan. In 2000 he became a player and part-owner of the Washington Wizards, and, in 2003, Jordan retired from the game.

Jackie Joyner-Kersee

Jackie Joyner-Kersee (1962–) is considered one of the world's top female athletes. Born in East Saint Louis, Joyner-Kersee has won a number of gold medals in track-and-field events at the Olympic Games.

Ray Kroc (1902–1984) of Chicago got the idea for a restaurant that served only hamburgers, french fries, and milkshakes from two California brothers named McDonald. He opened his first McDonald's in Des Plaines in 1955. From there, a chain of restaurants spread around the world. Today, "Hamburger U," where McDonald's trains its managers, is located in Oak Brook.

Abraham Lincoln (1809–1865) moved from Indiana to New Salem, Illinois, at age twenty-one. After studying law, Lincoln went to Springfield and opened his own law office. He served one term in the U.S. House of Representatives in the 1840s. He gained much fame through his debates with Stephen A. Douglas, whom he opposed in an unsuccessful bid for a U.S. Senate seat in 1858. In 1860 Lincoln was elected the sixteenth president of the United States. After leading the North through the Civil War, he was assassinated only days after the war's end.

Marlee Matlin (1965–), the first deaf person to win an Oscar for an acting role, was born in Morton Grove. Matlin won her Best Actress Oscar for her role in *Children of a Lesser God* in 1987. She was also the first deaf person to hold a leading role in a television series.

Carol Moseley Braun (1947–) became, in 1992, the first African-American woman to be elected to the U.S. Senate. She served ten years in the Illinois house of representatives before being chosen to serve in the U.S. Senate. She lost her Senate seat in 1998, was appointed U.S. ambassador to New Zealand and Samoa from 1999 to 2001, and joined the race in 2003 for the Democratic nomination for the presidential elections of 2004. Moseley Braun was born in Chicago.

Bill Murray (1950–), the popular comedian and actor, was born in Evanston. Murray came into the national spotlight with his role on *Saturday Night Live.* From television, he moved on to movies and starred in *Ghostbusters, Scrooged, Groundhog Day,* and *Lost in Translation.* Murray developed his talents with Chicago's famed Second City comedy theater company before joining the cast of *Saturday Night Live.*

Walter Payton

Walter Payton (1954–1999) was professional football's most successful running back. Born in Mississippi, Payton was drafted by the Chicago Bears in 1975. "Sweetness," as he was known, spent his entire thirteen-year career with the Bears and helped them win the Super Bowl in 1985. Payton held the record for most rushing yards by a running back.

Richard Peck (1934–), a noted children's writer, was born in Decatur. Peck's books for young adults cover sensitive issues such as suicide, pregnancy, and the death of a loved one. His books include *Remembering the Good Times* and *Ghosts I Have Been.* In 2001 he received the Newbery Award for *A Year Down Yonder.*

Ronald Reagan (1911–2004), who became the fortieth president of the United States, was born in Tampico. Reagan grew up in Dixon and attended Eureka College before moving to California and starting a career in acting. He served as governor of California before being elected president.

Carl Sandburg (1878–1967) was born in Galesburg and much of his writing concerned Illinois and the Midwest. He is well known for his six-volume biography of Abraham Lincoln and a number of poems including "Chicago," which gave the city its nickname, "The City of the Big Shoulders."

Shel Silverstein (1932–1999) from Chicago was famous for his popular children's books including *A Light in the Attic, Where the Sidewalk Ends,* and *The Giving Tree.* Silverstein wrote and illustrated his books.

Harold Washington (1922–1987) was born in Chicago and became the city's first African-American mayor. Washington served for many years in the Illinois legislature and then in the U.S. House of Representatives before being elected Chicago's mayor in 1983. He worked to bring women and minorities into city government.

Robin Williams (1952–) of Chicago has become one of America's best-loved comedians and actors. Known for his impersonations and zany style of comedy, Williams has appeared in many films including *Hook, Dead Poets Society, Mrs. Doubtfire* and won a best supporting Oscar for his role in *Good Will Hunting.*

Robin Williams

Oprah Winfrey (1954–) was born in Mississippi. In 1984 Winfrey accepted a job at a Chicago television station. Her talk show quickly became popular and before long was seen across the nation. Winfrey went on to star in movies, such as *The Color Purple,* and she is today one of America's wealthiest women.

TOUR THE STATE

Ulysses S. Grant Home State Historic Site (Galena) The people of Galena gave this house to Grant when he returned following the Civil War. It contains some of the Grants' original belongings.

John Deere Historic Site (Grand Detour) This historic site includes Deere's restored home and a reconstructed blacksmith shop.

Starved Rock State Park (La Salle) Starved Rock rises 125 feet into the air and is so named in memory of the group of Illinois Indians who made their last stand there and were wiped out because they lacked food and water.

Blackberry Historical Farm Village (Aurora) This reconstruction of an Illinois farm includes guides dressed in period costume and a Discovery Barn with farm animals.

McDonald's Museum (Des Plaines) The museum is built on the site of the original 1955 restaurant and tells the story of the popular eating place.

Brookfield Zoo (Brookfield) This large zoo holds mammals, reptiles, and birds in cageless areas that resemble their natural habitats.

Hull House (Chicago) Jane Addams's famous settlement house has been restored; exhibits found inside show the history of the neighborhood.

Chicago Children's Museum (Chicago) This fun museum has exhibits on garbage and Legos.

The Field Museum (Chicago) This huge natural sciences museum contains exhibits on everything from gems and ancient Egypt to dinosaurs.

John G. Shedd Aquarium (Chicago) More than six thousand freshwater and marine animals, including whales and dolphins, can be found there.

Sears Tower (Chicago) Visitors to one of the world's tallest buildings can view the city from the observation deck on the 103rd floor.

Lincoln's New Salem Historic Site (Petersburg) The town where Abraham Lincoln lived from 1831–1837 is reconstructed at this site.

Lincoln Home National Historic Site (Springfield) The house found at this location is the only home Lincoln ever owned.

Lincoln's Tomb State Historic Site (Springfield) Abraham Lincoln, Mrs. Lincoln, and three of the four Lincoln children are buried in this beautiful monument.

Illinois State Museum (Springfield) Three floors of exhibits showcase Illinois's natural history as well as the history of the state's Native Americans and settlers.

Giant City State Park (Carbondale) Huge blocks of stone rise from the canyons of this rugged park.

Fort de Chartres State Historic Site (Prairie du Rocher) The stone buildings at this site are an imitation of those found in the 1760s when Fort de Chartres was a French settlement in the Illinois country.

Cahokia Mounds State Historic Site (Collinsville) Cahokia Mounds is the site of a city inhabited by people of the Mississippian culture from 900 to 1500 C.E. Sixty-five mounds still exist, the largest standing more than 100 feet tall.

Cahokia Courthouse State Historic Site (Cahokia) The courthouse was built in 1737 as a French home and is the oldest building in Illinois.

Joseph Smith Historic Center (Nauvoo) Several buildings related to the town's Mormon past are found at this site.

Fort Crèvecoeur Park (Peoria) A reconstruction of the fort built in 1680 by La Salle near a Peoria Indian village is found there.

Wildlife Prairie Park (Peoria) Bison, elk, wolves, and bears can be seen on the 2,000 acres of preserved prairie.

Mississippi River Visitor Center (Rock Island) Visitors can learn a lot about river travel as well as watch boats pass through the locks on the Mississippi.

FUN FACTS

One lesser known nickname for Illinois is the "Sucker State." No one is sure where this name came from. Some people think it goes back to the days when Illinois was just being settled. Crawfish in the area burrowed into the ground, creating small holes that often filled up with fresh water. Pioneers could then suck up the water from the holes, which they called suckers.

On September 10, 1890, a shower of fish fell on the town of Cairo. No explanation has ever been given for the event.

The game of pinball was invented by Chicago's In and Outdoor Games Company in 1930.

Robert Wadlow, born in Alton in 1918, was the tallest man in the world. Wadlow stood 8 feet 11 inches tall, weighed 491 pounds (although he looked thin), and wore a size 37 shoe.

Find Out More

If you'd like to find out more about Illinois, look in your school library, local library, bookstore, or video store. Here are some titles to ask for:

GENERAL STATE BOOKS

Fradin, Dennis. *Illinois*. Chicago: Childrens Press, 1994.

Marsh, Carole. *Illinois Quiz Bowl Crash Course!* Decatur, GA: Gallopade Publishing, 1992.

Schuldt, Lori Meek. *Fun with the Family in Illinois*. Augusta, GA: Globe Pequot, 2004.

Wills, Charles. *The Historical Album of Illinois*. Brookfield, CT: Millbrook Press, 1994.

SPECIAL ILLINOIS PEOPLE AND INTEREST BOOKS

Beaton, Margaret. *Oprah Winfrey: TV Talk Show Host*. Chicago: Childrens Press, 1990.

Bial, Ray. *Portrait of a Farm Family*. New York: Houghton Mifflin, 1995.

———. *Visit to Amish Country*. New York: Houghton Mifflin, 1995.

Brooks, Gwendolyn. *Children Coming Home*. Chicago: Gwendolyn Brooks, 1991.

Cumpian, Carlos. *Latino Rainbow*. Chicago: Childrens Press, 1994. (biographies in verse about well-known Latinos, including many Illinoisans)

Kent, Deborah. *Jane Addams and Hull House*. Chicago: Childrens Press, 1992.

Macy, Sue. *A Whole New Ball Game*. New York: Henry Holt, 1993. (about the women's baseball league)

Marsh, Carole. *Illinois Pirates, Bandits, Bushwackers, Outlaws, Crooks, Devils, Ghosts, Desperadoes, Rogues, Heroes, and Other Assorted & Sundry Characters*. Decatur, GA: Gallopade Publishing, 1990.

Sandburg, Carl. *Rootabaga Stories. The Sandburg Treasury: Prose and Poetry for Young People*. New York: Harcourt Brace Jovanovich, 1956. (selections from biographies of Sandburg and Abraham Lincoln and poems about Illinois)

VIDEOTAPES

"Michael Jordan: Come Fly with Me." New York: CBS Fox Video Sports, 1989.

"Illinois Historic Panorama, Overview." Macomb, IL: WIU/ISBE Satellite Education Network, Western Illinois University, 1991.

WEB SITES

The Official State Web Site
http://www.illinois.gov/

Discover Illinois: Kids Zone
http://www.state.il.us/kids/

Illinois Department of Agriculture Kids Page
http://www.agr.state.il.us/kidspage/

The Illinois History Research Page
http://www.historyillinois.org/hist.html
Go to the "Just for Kids" section, for additional links.

INDEX

Page numbers in **boldface** are illustrations and charts.

ABOUT THE AUTHOR

Marlene Targ Brill's background as a special education teacher led to her interest in writing. She has written articles on a wide range of topics, many fiction and nonfiction books for young readers, and award-winning educational materials for parents.

The author lives in Wilmette, Illinois, with her husband, Richard, and daughter, Alison. She traveled from one end of the state to the other to write this book.